IMPERIUM

IN

IMPERIO

SUTTON E. GRIGGS

IMPERIUM
IN
IMPERIO

Preface by A. J. Verdelle

Introduction by Cornel West

THE MODERN LIBRARY

NEW YORK

2/28/05

2003 Modern Library Paperback Edition

Introduction and chronology copyright © 2003 by Cornel West
Preface copyright © 2003 by A. J. Verdelle
Reading group guide © 2003 by Random House, Inc.

LIBRARY OF CONGRESS CATALOGING-IN-PUBLICATION DATA
Griggs, Sutton Elbert, 1872–
Imperium in imperio/Sutton E. Griggs; introduction by Cornel West; preface by
A. J. Verdelle.—2003 Modern library pbk. ed.
p.   cm.
ISBN 0-8129-7160-4
1. Racially mixed people—Fiction.   2. African American men—Fiction.
3. Black nationalism—Fiction.   4. Radicals—Fiction.   5. Racism—Fiction.
6. Texas—Fiction.   I. Title.

PS3513.R7154I56 2003
813'.52—dc22   2003044282

Modern Library website address: www.modernlibrary.com

Printed in the United States of America

2 4 6 8 9 7 5 3 1

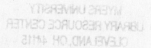

CONTENTS

IMPERIUM IN IMPERIO

PREFACE

A. J. Verdelle

All of Sutton Griggs's work—five novels, and more than twenty other texts: political and religious, autobiographical essays and sermons—focuses on the problem of race in America. Griggs, like many of his countrymen and contemporaries, was consumed by the riotous race climate in this young country, inflamed by the race inequities on which this nation was birthed. The race calamity that was America demanded devotion and attention from Negroes alive and thinking during the post-Emancipation years. The reigning positions on Negroes needed constant proving wrong. Sutton Griggs took up this charge, like writers Paul Laurence Dunbar, Charles Chesnutt, and Frances Harper; scholar William Edward Burkhardt Du Bois; and contemporary writers, scholars, and artists who will march into the future, from Reconstruction forward.

Griggs devoted his work, his life, his very breath to the question of race in America. He wrote to reveal, to shine a light on, to identify absent protections and other race problems. He wrote to consider, or to reconsider, these imposed implications of skin.

In the African-American church, the word *tireless* is often used as high accolade. Griggs's efforts on behalf of his race were tireless.

—

Sutton Griggs's first novel, *Imperium in Imperio* (1899), presents a tale of a secret and radical separate Negro government, or a secret society, told by way of two contemporaries. This kind of character arrangement was often used in nineteenth-century literature—often with one "son" of the story being fine and good, and the other being the personification of some opposite, some evil. The characters' divergence, their fractious meetings, their imbalanced fortunes, their differing fates—all serve as the story's events. African-American literature from this period often makes both characters heroes of the tale—both Negroes being good, well motivated, respectable, but with one whose life is more doomed than the other's.

Sutton Griggs, in *Imperium*, introduces his doubly heroic pair and makes them "brothers in the struggle" as the story goes along. Born on the cusp of national law against slavery, and born to opposite circumstances, Griggs's heroes—Belton Piedmont and Bernard Belgrave—are both steel-willed characters, determined to confront the heat and pressure of their time and caste. Young men, race men, free men, antebellum men—Piedmont and Belgrave are reunited in the narrative to bring a partnered, collected intelligence to bear on the crises at hand. Causes burn fiercely during Reconstruction. The bright promises of freedom demand strong action and require courage and will to agitate for change.

Griggs's heroes are typical of the Reconstructionists. At the end of the nineteenth century, there were African-American senators in Congress! This political reality was not repeated for scores of years. Reconstructionists were men—newly free—who had every intention of stepping up to the lectern from which freedom's high praises were spoken. Reconstruction—the great reorganization after slavery—was expected to birth results far more favorable than what history has proved.

Writing as Reconstruction moved from plan to practice, Griggs presented the world as he lived it in the novels he wrote. *Imperium's* first hero, Piedmont, a dark man, is destined for the hardest knocks and most visible labor. Belgrave, a lighter man with comparable intelligence and dedication, is destined for better training, for leadership, for higher heights.

Fateful color differences aside, both Belgrave and Piedmont, like Griggs and his contemporaries, are hungry intellectuals. In the nineteenth century, the Negro intellectual *is starving*, literally and literarily, for the competence and communion that only education affords. Intellectual atrophy, or starvation, creates a gaping feeling: a hunger unyielding, a big muscle unused.

Griggs and his contemporaries cast their characters adrift in this boiling cauldron of stone soup. Intellectual malnutrition, planned and enforced. (Consider the children of this diet.) The status quo when Sutton Griggs lived, without freedoms adequate to his birthright, withheld knowledge of all kinds from Negroes—slaves and manumitted men alike. This brutish claim on knowledge was high moral crime.

———

Perhaps the ring of that famous slogan to come—*A mind is a terrible thing to waste*—begins to sound (in some other arrangement of words) to those who assembled as Sutton Griggs, writer and preacher, spread his message. This expression exactly represents the position that Sutton Griggs and his contemporaries took: *A mind is a terrible thing to waste.*

Of all the outcomes, the legacies, the continuing curses of slavery, Free Men knew Above All that they needed to reclaim, and redeem, and resuscitate the Life of the Negro Mind. Slavery dulled the mind and enflamed the senses of its subjects. Slavery sullied the moral character and dulled the senses of its perpetrators. Negro writers, thinkers, philosophers, pastors, scholars—like Griggs on one end of social and scholarly acceptance and Du Bois at another—campaigned to defend, glorify, politicize, and activate the mental skills of the Race, to be permitted to nurture, use, and make public presentation of the minds God gave them.

———

Negro intellectual redemption and how this should be ushered in was a hot topic during Reconstruction: first belabored in secret, in stolen assembly, where one renegade taught another, maybe to mark key characters, like P-A-S-S. As the portal to education—to texts and to script—began to open and let in a little light, American Negro leadership took shape in earnest. Griggs claimed a place in this group.

Like others of his ilk, his caliber—men who read, who wrote, who endeavored to educate, who stood before audiences—Sutton Griggs unceasingly testified to the abilities of the Negro race. *We are Men, mentally capable, mentally competent.* To have to repeatedly make such an assertion, to devote one's life and energies to proving such an idea, is a mind-boggling undertaking. Griggs was only one of a very famous many who devoted their skills and their lives to this redemption.

W.E.B. Du Bois and Booker T. Washington had an historic, long-term, and very public disagreement on this very subject: What is the best and most expedient strategy for nourishing hungry Negro minds? Washington firmly believed in the idea of the lumpen Negro, and felt that all Negroes should receive industrial education. According to Washington, any special placements or investigations of higher power should be foregone. Industrial education for all! Washington argued that Negro political struggles should be *suspended* (as if this was possible, feasible, as if this monolithic goal could be attained), while the industrial education of every Negro worked its kind of repair.

Du Bois considered that at least some portion of the race (his "talented tenth") should receive special, advanced education, so that they could prepare and lead Negroes into modern civilization. Here Du Bois takes an early position against the monolithic Negro population. One color, one plan, one strategy—this seemed to be the lumpen argument that Du Bois refused to accept.

By the example of *Imperium*, Griggs weighs in on the Du Bois side of the argument. *Imperium* as a story follows the path of the educated Negro. The novel presents Griggs's notion of the commanding, fine, proactive, forward-thinking citizens universities can help create. Du Bois's notion of education and agitation is apparent in *Imperium*: Griggs bluntly presents "reconstructionists for a cause."

Griggs chronicles men who were custodians of an era—undertaking reconstruction was work with importance beyond measure. The story of the spurned and uncrowned intellectuals, their efforts, their pleas, their rages, their societies, collegiality, their industry—this is what the late nineteenth century wrought. These machinations made the twentieth century and thereafter possible, made Negroes from slaves, who then become Black and then, in a far future, African American. Sutton Griggs and his contemporaries were committed to learn and read and thrive, to re-name, survive, to reclaim full use of the mental territories made so fully off limits, and to enter the personal intellectual geographies so viciously and aggressively denied.

———

Time and criticism have sometimes been harsh to Sutton Griggs. His work has been ignored, and when it has been considered or visible, he has often been labeled polemical. Some vacillation in Griggs's positions has been observed—from writing radical novels and tracts, to presenting positions that seem accommodationist (instances where he seemed more Washington, and less Du Bois). Because of this shifting, even across works of fiction, it seems, Griggs has been labeled "uncertain," which is not high praise.

No matter the labels assigned, however, Griggs was an important minor novelist writing at an exceedingly important time. His record of the cauldron of pressures and hungers is worthy as history, as a record of a Negro's extreme vulnerability during that time, even on the most quotidian front. One of the heroes in this novel was actually lynched. In the true fantastic fashion of fiction, the hero lives to tell the story. Lynching was a common, everyday worry during the first years after Abolition. To be faced with the constant threat of lynching or other mob action is a very hard fear to fathom, and yet, for Sutton Griggs and all people of his color, this fear was bald fact.

With the publication of *Imperium in Imperio,* Griggs has been credited, however quietly, with writing the first political novel by a black American. This is no small credit. On occasion, Griggs has also been linked to the ideas of the New Negro, which, in a few years forward, the Harlem Renaissance would usher in with aplomb. Griggs's work has also been tied to 1960s' militant philosophies and practices. Both of these suggested relationships celebrate Griggs's accomplishments, without arguing that his work or his positions were abundantly clear across the entire oeuvre.

Sutton E. Griggs managed to emerge into prosperity with a literary reputation, despite limited artistic skills and work that he published and sold himself, often as he traveled on organizational business for his church. Griggs's contemporary Charles Chesnutt is widely held as the first African-American novelist to write artistically, with attention to fictional technique. Nonetheless, Griggs is credited with having a potentially wider readership than either Dunbar or Chesnutt, because he did not rely on publishers and was willing to sell his work directly to the public. No publishing institutions were necessary to intervene or impede.

Griggs was a strategist, a true citizen of the era of Reconstruction. After the vise and grip of slavery were loosened, those who felt able gave their attention to thinking through the most pressing race problems. Men and women of the race convened to consider, debate, and advance strategies.

Sutton E. Griggs—writer, pastor, strategist, and child of a mother whose name is lost to history—counted himself among the inheritors of a new and sanctioned space. Reading, writing, and study were prohibited for Negroes in America by law. Sutton E. Griggs lived during the advent of the first legal uses of the Negro mind. *Imperium in Imperio,* for all else that this novel is and is not, presents a fine example of the baroque lengths to which the new Negro thinkers and writers extended themselves, trying to enter a new age in a promised partnership with this oppressor nation.

——

A. J. VERDELLE, lecturer in the creative writing program at Princeton, is the author of *The Good Negress.*

INTRODUCTION

Cornel West

Sutton Elbert Griggs was one of the most significant black public intellectuals at the turn of the twentieth century. He wrote and spoke with great courage and wisdom about black dignity and suffering during the age of American imperialism (Philippines, Cuba, et al.) and U.S. terrorism (Jim Crow, lynching). His works constitute a beacon of light during the night years of the nadir of modern black history.

Griggs was one of the most precocious writers of his generation. Born in Chatfield, Texas, in 1872, he graduated from Bishop College in Marshall, Texas, at the age of eighteen and completed Richmond Theological Seminary at twenty-one. Like his well-known father, Allen R. Griggs, he became a Baptist pastor and led churches in Virginia, Tennessee, and Texas, including Hopewell Baptist Church, a post held by his father. He published his most important novel, *Imperium in Imperio,* at the age of twenty-seven—two years after his marriage to Emma J. Williams of Portsmouth, Virginia, and five years after he accepted the pastorate of historic First

Baptist Church in East Nashville, Tennessee. He died at the age of sixty after publishing more than forty texts, though he remains relatively unknown today. What a shame!

This publication is a grand effort to rectify the unwarranted neglect of Griggs. His life and works deserve serious attention and examination. *Imperium in Imperio* (1899) is the first major political novel written by an African American. It is the first literary portrait of a black revolutionary movement in violent revolt against white supremacist America. As his black character Belton Piedmont proclaims:

> The cringing, fawning, sniffling, cowardly Negro which slavery left, had disappeared, and a new Negro, self-respecting, fearless, and determined in the assertion of his rights was at hand.

Overshadowed (1901) is the first literary indictment of the global scope of white supremacy (European imperialism in Africa and U.S. Jim Crowism at home). *Unfettered* (1902) deals with the overlooked phenomenon of black love against the background of protracted black enhancement. *The Hindered Hand* (1905) examines miscegenation, lynching, and back-to-Africa efforts. And his last novel, *Pointing the Way* (1908), posits the courts as the most effective strategy for black progress.

Griggs's numerous political works—from *The Race Question in a New Light* (1909) to *The Guide to Racial Greatness* (1923)—highlight not only strategies for black political elevation but also the beauty, intelligence, and character of black people. Like the great filmmaker and author Oscar Micheaux, Griggs published his own works and often sold them door-to-door. Furthermore, Griggs was one of the most powerful orators of his day. As a political activist and passionate communicator, Griggs had a tremendous impact on his audiences.

In short, Sutton Griggs was an exemplary Christian humanist

who conveyed to the world his own distinctive quest for *sapientia* (wisdom), *eloquentia* (eloquence), and *prudentia* (prudence) in Jim Crow America. His fundamental assumption of the humanity of black people was a revolutionary idea in a white supremacist civilization. This idea was attacked in the bestsellers of the day—Thomas Nelson Page's *Red Rock* (1898) and Thomas Dixon Jr.'s *The Clansman: An Historical Romance of the Ku Klux Klan* (1905). The latter was transformed by D. W. Griffith into *The Birth of a Nation* (1916)—the *Matrix* of its day, with unprecedented popularity and celebration. Page, Dixon, and Griffith contributed greatly to the notion that black people were inferior and deserved their subjugation—the very idea Griggs spent his life contesting and undermining.

Griggs also enacted an honest form of self-examination that accented the white supremacy in black people. When he raises the basic question, at the end of *Imperium in Imperio:* "When will all races and classes of men learn that men made in the image of God will not be the slaves of another image?" Griggs directs it at both black and white Americans. He connects the courage to think critically with the courage to fight valiantly; and he knows that black dogma trumps the former and black cowardice precludes the latter. Despite his artistic lapses and literary limitations, Griggs presents black despair and black hope against hope in a powerful and poignant manner.

Hence his relevance for us today at the turn of another century. Our time is marked by imperial ventures, domestic repression, wealth inequality, and continuing racial division. The witness and work of Sutton Elbert Griggs constitute a grand example that the exercise of vision, intelligence, courage, and love are never in vain—even among a hated black people in an American empire haunted by its past and present crimes against humanity.

———

CORNEL WEST is currently the Class of 1943 University Professor of Religion at Princeton University, teaching various courses for the Department of Religion and African American Studies Program. He is the author of numerous articles and books. His book credits include *Race Matters, The Cornel West Reader, Prophetic Fragments, Restoring Hope, Prophesy Deliverance, The American Evasion of Philosophy, Keeping Faith, The Ethical Dimensions of Marxist Thought, Prophetic Reflections,* and *Prophetic Thought in Postmodern Times.*

Chronology of the Precocious Sutton E. Griggs

1872 Born of father, Allen R. Griggs, and of a mother whose name was unrecorded, on June 19, in Chatfield, Texas.

1890 Graduates Bishop College, Marshall, Texas (age 18).

1893 Graduates Richmond Theological Seminary (age 21).

1896 Griggs begins thirty years in Tennessee. Pastor at First Baptist Church of East Nashville, and then nineteen years as pastor of the Tabernacle Baptist Church of Memphis.

1897 Marries Emma J. Williams of Portsmouth, Virginia; no children (age 25).

1899 *Imperium in Imperio.* Political novel, self-published, considered Griggs's best and most important work of fiction (age 27).

1901 *Overshadowed.* Second political novel that focused on conditions created by segregation (age 29).

1902 *Unfettered.* Love story between a mulatta and a courageous Negro hero who develops a plan for elevating the black race. This fifty-page plan is fully conceived, written with judicious seriousness, and appears in the novel as an appendix (age 30).

1905 *The Hindered Hand.* Griggs's fourth novel, about American oppressions of the Negro and emigration to Africa, which is explored as a solution (age 33).

1908 *Pointing the Way.* Griggs's fifth novel, a treatment of legal action as possible recourse for blacks. A strategy that the future bears out so completely that Griggs's suggestion or foresight seems almost portentous (age 36).

1909 Griggs abandons the novel as a form and begins to publish tracts—political and social—in which he continues to examine the most weighty Negro problems, including lynching, black suffrage, and inadequate opportunities for employment. The most well known of these works is *The Guide to Racial Greatness* (1923), which attempts to solve many of the problems lived by Negroes in America at the time and explored in Griggs's fiction.

1933 Dies, Houston, Texas, on January 5, while immersed in a project to found a religious and civic institute (age 60).

1940s Griggs's works come out of obscurity and become subjects of scholarly and critical attention, and his political visions are debated.

A Note on the Text

This Modern Library Paperback Classic is set from the text of the first edition of *Imperium in Imperio*, published in 1899 by The Editor Publishing Co. of Cincinnati.

IMPERIUM

IN

IMPERIO

To the Public

The papers which are herewith submitted to you for your perusal and consideration, were delivered into my hands by Mr. Berl Trout.

The papers will speak for themselves, but Mr. Trout now being dead I feel called upon to say a word concerning him.

Mr. Berl Trout was Secretary of State in the Imperium In Imperio, from the day of its organization until the hour of his sad death. He was, therefore, thoroughly conversant with all of the details of that great organization.

He was a warm personal friend of both Bernard and Belton, and learned from their own lips the stories of their eventful lives.

Mr. Trout was a man noted for his strict veracity and for the absolute control that his conscience exercised over him.

Though unacquainted with the Imperium In Imperio I was well acquainted with Berl, as we fondly called him. I will vouch for his truthfulness anywhere.

Having perfect faith in the truthfulness of his narrative I have not hesitated to fulfil his dying request by editing his Ms., and giving it to the public. There are other documents in my possession tending to confirm the assertions made in his narrative. These documents were given me by Mr. Trout, so that, in case an attempt is made to pronounce him a liar, I might defend his name by coming forward with indisputable proofs of every important statement.

Very respectfully,
Sutton E. Griggs,
Berkley, Va.
March 1, 1899.

Berl Trout's
Dying Declaration

I am a traitor. I have violated an oath that was as solemn and binding as any ever taken by man on earth.

I have trampled under my feet the sacred trust of a loving people, and have betrayed secrets which were dearer to them than life itself.

For this offence, regarded the world over as the most detestable of horrors, I shall be slain.

Those who shall be detailed to escort my foul body to its grave are required to walk backwards with heads averted.

On to-morrow night, the time of my burial, the clouds should gather thick about the queenly moon to hide my funeral procession from her view, for fear that she might refuse to longer reign over a land capable of producing such a wretch as I.

In the bottom of some old forsaken well, so reads *our* law, I shall be buried, face downward, without a coffin; and my body, lying thus, will be transfixed with a wooden stave.

Fifty feet from the well into which my body is lowered, a red flag is to be hoisted and kept floating there for time unending, to warn all generations of men to come not near the air polluted by the rotting carcass of a vile traitor.

Such is my fate. I seek not to shun it. I have walked into odium with every sense alert, fully conscious of every step taken.

While I acknowledge that I am a traitor, I also pronounce myself a patriot.

It is true that I have betrayed the immediate plans of the race to which I belong; but I have done this in the interest of the whole human family—of which my race is but a part.

My race may, for the time being, shower curses upon me; but eventually all races, including my own, shall call me blessed.

The earth, in anger, may belch forth my putrid flesh with volcanic fury, but the out-stretched arms of God will receive my spirit as a token of approval of what I have done.

With my soul feasting on this happy thought, I send this revelation to mankind and yield my body to the executioner to be shot until I am dead.

Though death stands just before me, holding before my eyes my intended shroud woven of the cloth of infamy itself, I shrink not back.

Yours, doomed to die,
BERL TROUT.

CHAPTER I

A SMALL BEGINNING

"Cum er long hunny an' let yer mammy fix yer 'spectabul, so yer ken go to skule. Yer mammy is 'tarmined ter gib yer all de book larning dar is ter be had eben ef she has ter lib on bred an' herrin's, an' die en de a'ms house."

These words came from the lips of a poor, ignorant negro woman, and yet the determined course of action which they reveal vitally affected the destiny of a nation and saved the sun of the Nineteenth Century, proud and glorious, from passing through, near its setting, the blackest and thickest and ugliest clouds of all its journey; saved it from ending the most brilliant of brilliant careers by setting, with a shudder of horror, in a sea of human blood.

Those who doubt that such power could emanate from such weakness; or, to change the figure, that such a tiny star could have dimensions greater than those of earth, may have every vestige of doubt removed by a perusal of this simple narrative.

Let us now acquaint ourselves with the circumstances under which the opening words of our story were spoken. To do this, we must need lead our readers into humble and commonplace surroundings, a fact that will not come in the nature of a surprise to those who have traced the proud, rushing, swelling river to the mountain whence it comes trickling forth, meekly and humbly enough.

The place was Winchester, an antiquated town, located near the northwestern corner of the State of Virginia.

In October of the year 1867, the year in which our story begins, a white man by the name of Tiberius Gracchus Leonard had arrived in Winchester, and was employed as teacher of the school for colored children.

Mrs. Hannah Piedmont, the colored woman whom we have presented to our readers as addressing her little boy, was the mother of five children,—three girls and two boys. In the order of their ages, the names of her children were: James Henry, aged fifteen, Amanda Ann, aged thirteen, Eliza Jane, aged eleven, Belton, aged eight, and Celestine, aged five. Several years previous to the opening of our history, Mr. Piedmont had abandoned his wife and left her to rear the children alone.

School opened in October, and as fast as she could get books and clothing Mrs. Piedmont sent her children to school. James Henry, Amanda Ann, and Eliza Jane were sent at about a week's interval. Belton and Celestine were then left—Celestine being regarded as too young to go. This morning we find Belton's mother preparing him for school, and we shall stand by and watch the preparations.

The house was low and squatty and was built of rock. It consisted of one room only, and over this there was a loft, the hole to climb into which was in plain view of any one in the room. There was only one window to the house and that one was only four feet square. Two panes of this were broken out and the holes were stuffed with rags. In one corner of the room there stood a bed in which Mrs. Piedmont and Amanda Ann slept. Under this was a trundle bed in which Eliza Jane and Celestine slept at the head, while Belton slept at the foot. James Henry climbed into the loft and slept there on a pallet of straw. The cooking was done in a fireplace which was on the side of the house opposite the window. Three chairs, two of which had no backs to them, completed the articles in the room.

In one of these chairs Mrs. Piedmont was sitting, while Belton stood before her all dressed and ready to go to school, excepting that his face was not washed.

It might be interesting to note his costume. The white lady for whom Mrs. Piedmont washed each week had given her two much-torn pairs of trousers, discarded by her young son. One pair was of linen and the other of navy blue. A leg from each pair was missing; so Mrs. Piedmont simply transferred the good leg of the linen pair to the suit of the navy blue, and dressed the happy Belton in that suit thus amended. His coat was literally a conglomeration of patches of varying sizes and colors. If you attempted to describe the coat by calling it by the name of the color that you thought predominated, at least a half dozen aspirants could present equal claims to the honor. One of Belton's feet was encased in a wornout slipper from the dainty foot of some young woman, while the other wore a turned over boot left in town by some farmer lad who had gotten himself a new pair. His hat was in good condition, being the summer straw last worn by a little white playfellow (when fall came on, this little fellow kindly willed his hat to Belton, who, in return for this favor, was to black the boy's shoes each morning during the winter).

Belton's mother now held in her hand a wet cloth with which she wished to cleanse his face, the bacon skin which he gnawed at the conclusion of his meal having left a circle of grease around his lips. Belton did not relish the face washing part of the programme (of course hair combing was not even considered). Belton had one characteristic similar to that of oil. He did not like to mix with water, especially cold water, such as was on that wet cloth in his mother's hand. However, a hint in reference to a certain well-known leather strap, combined with the offer of a lump of sugar, brought him to terms.

His face being washed, he and his mother marched forth to school, where he laid the foundation of the education that served him so well in after life.

A man of tact, intelligence, and superior education moving in the midst of a mass of ignorant people, ofttimes has a sway more absolute than that of monarchs. *Shows the importance of education—Seper* *fsm*

Belton now entered the school-room, which in his case proves to be the royal court, whence he emerges an uncrowned king.

CHAPTER II

THE SCHOOL

The house in which the colored school was held was, in former times, a house of worship for the white Baptists of Winchester. It was a long, plain, frame structure, painted white. Many years prior to the opening of the colored school it had been condemned as unsafe by the town authorities, whereupon the white Baptists had abandoned it for a more beautiful modern structure.

The church tendered the use of the building to the town for a public school for the colored children. The roof was patched and iron rods were used to hold together the twisting walls. These improvements being made, school was in due time opened. The building was located on the outskirts of the town, and a large open field surrounded it on all sides.

As Mrs. Piedmont and her son drew near to this building the teacher was standing on the door-steps ringing his little hand bell, calling the children in from their recess. They came running at full speed, helter skelter. By the time they were all in Mrs. Piedmont and Belton had arrived at the step. When Mr. Leonard saw them about to enter the building an angry scowl passed over his face, and he muttered half aloud: "Another black nigger brat for me to teach."

The steps were about four feet high and he was standing on the top step. To emphasize his disgust, he drew back so that Mrs. Piedmont would pass him with no danger of brushing him. He drew back rather too far and began falling off the end of the steps. He clutched at the door and made such a scrambling noise that the children turned in their seats just in time to see his body rapidly disappearing in a manner to leave his feet where his head ought to be.

Such a yell of laughter as went up from the throats of the children! It had in it a universal, spontaneous ring of savage delight which plainly told that the teacher was not beloved by his pupils.

The back of the teacher's head struck the edge of a stone, and when he clambered up from his rather undignified position his back was covered with blood. Deep silence reigned in the school-room as he walked down the aisle, glaring fiercely right and left. Getting his hat he left the school-room and went to a near-by drug store to have his wounds dressed.

While he was gone, the children took charge of the school-room and played pranks of every description. Abe Lincoln took the teacher's chair and played " 'fessor."

"Sallie Ann ain't yer got wax in yer mouf?"

"Yes sar."

"Den take dis stick and prop yer mouf opun fur half hour. Dat'll teach yer a lesson."

"Billy Smith, yer didn't know yer lessun," says teacher Abe. "Yer may stan' on one leg de ballunce ob de ebenning."

"Henry Jones, yer sassed a white boy ter day. Pull off yer jacket. I'll gib yer a lessun dat yer'll not furgit soon. Neber buck up to yer s'periors."

"John Jones, yer black, nappy head rascal, I'll crack yer skull if yer doan keep quiut."

"Cum year, yer black, cross-eyed little wench, yer. I'll teach yer to go to sleep in here." Annie Moore was the little girl thus addressed.

After each sally from Abe there was a hearty roar of laughter, he imitated the absent teacher so perfectly in look, voice, manner, sentiment, and method of punishment.

Taking down the cowhide used for flogging purposes Abe left his seat and was passing to and fro, pretending to flog those who most frequently fell heir to the teacher's wrath. While he was doing this Billy Smith stealthily crept to the teacher's chair and placed a crooked pin in it in order to catch Abe when he returned to sit down.

Before Abe had gone much further the teacher's face appeared at the door, and all scrambled to get into their right places and to assume studious attitudes. Billy Smith thought of his crooked pin and had the "cold sweats." Those who had seen Billy put the pin in the chair were torn between two conflicting emotions. They wanted the pin to do its work, and therefore hoped. They feared Billy's detection and therefore despaired.

However, the teacher did not proceed at once to take his seat. He approached Mrs. Piedmont and Belton, who had taken seats midway the room and were interested spectators of all that had been going on. Speaking to Mrs. Piedmont, he said: "What is your name?"

She replied: "Hannah Lizabeth Piedmont."

"Well, Hannah, what is your brat's name?"

"His name am Belton Piedmont, arter his grandaddy."

"Well, Hannah, I am very pleased to receive your brat. He shall not want for attention," he added, in a tone accompanied by a lurking look of hate that made Mrs. Piedmont shudder and long to have her boy at home again. Her desire for his training was so great that she surmounted her misgivings and carried out her purposes to have him enrolled.

As the teacher was turning to go to his desk, hearing a rustling noise toward the door, he turned to look. He was, so to speak, petrified with astonishment. There stood on the threshold of the door a woman whose beauty was such as he had never seen surpassed. She held a boy by the hand. She was a mulatto woman, tall and graceful. Her hair was raven black and was combed away from as beautiful a forehead as nature could chisel. Her eyes were a brown hazel, large and intelligent, tinged with a slight look of melancholy. Her complexion was a rich olive, and seemed especially adapted to her face, that revealed not a flaw.

The teacher quickly pulled off his hat, which he had not up to that time removed since his return from the drug store. As the lady moved up the aisle toward him, he was taken with stage fright. He recovered self-possession enough to escort her and the boy to the front and give them seats. The whole school divided its attention between the beautiful woman and the discomfitted teacher. They had not known that he was so full of smiles and smirks.

"What is your name?" he enquired in his most suave manner.

"Fairfax Belgrave," replied the visitor.

"May I be of any service to you, madam?"

At the mention of the word *madam,* she colored slightly. "I desire to have my son enter your school and I trust that you may see your way clear to admit him."

"Most assuredly madam, most assuredly." Saying this, he hastened to his desk, opened it and took out his register. He then sat down, but the next instant leapt several feet into the air, knocking over his desk. He danced around the floor, reaching toward the rear of his pants, yelling: "Pull it out! pull it out! pull it out!"

The children hid their faces behind their books and chuckled most gleefully. Billy Smith was struck dumb with terror. Abe was rolling on the floor, bellowing with uncontrollable laughter.

The teacher finally succeeded in extricating the offending steel and stood scratching his head in chagrin at the spectacle he had made of himself before his charming visitor. He took an internal oath to get his revenge out of Mrs. Piedmont and her son, who had been the innocent means of his double downfall that day.

His desk was arranged in a proper manner and the teacher took his pen and wrote two names, now famous the world over.

"Bernard Belgrave, age 9 years."

"Belton Piedmont, age 8 years."

Under such circumstances Belton began his school career.

CHAPTER III

The Parson's Advice

With heavy heart and with eyes cast upon the ground, Mrs. Piedmont walked back home after leaving Belton with his teacher. She had intended to make a special plea for her boy, who had all along displayed such precociousness as to fill her bosom with the liveliest hopes. But the teacher was so repulsive in manner that she did not have the heart to speak to him as she had intended.

She saw that the happenings of the morning had had the effect of deepening a contemptuous prejudice into hatred, and she felt that her child's school life was to be embittered by the harshest of maltreatment.

No restraint was put upon the flogging of colored children by their white teachers, and in Belton's case his mother expected the worst. During the whole week she revolved the matter in her mind. There was a conflict in her bosom between her love and her ambition. Love prompted her to return and take her son away from school. Ambition bade her to let him stay. She finally decided to submit the whole matter to her parson, whom she would invite to dinner on the coming Sunday.

The Sabbath came and Mrs. Piedmont aroused her family bright and early, for the coming of the parson to take dinner was a great event in any negro household. The house was swept as clean as a broom of weeds tied together could make it. Along with the family breakfast, a skillet of biscuits was cooked and a young chicken nicely baked.

Belton was very active in helping his mother that morning, and she promised to give him a biscuit and a piece of chicken as a reward after the preacher was through eating his dinner. The thought of this coming happiness buoyed Belton up, and often he fancied himself munching that biscuit and biting that piece of chicken. These were items of food rarely found in that household.

Breakfast over, the whole family made preparations for going to Sunday school. Preparations always went on peacefully until it came to combing hair. The older members of the family endured the ordeal very well; but little "Lessie" always screamed as if she was being tortured, and James Henry received many kicks and scratches from Belton before he was through combing Belton's hair.

The Sunday school and church were always held in the day-school building. The Sunday school scholars were all in one class and recited out of the "blue back spelling book." When that was over, members of the school were allowed to ask general questions on the Bible, which were answered by anyone volunteering to do so. Everyone who had in any way caught a new light on a passage of scripture endeavored, by questioning, to find out as to whether others were as wise as he, and if such was not the case, he gladly enlightened the rest.

The Sunday school being over, the people stood in groups on the ground surrounding the church waiting for the arrival of the parson from his home, Berryville, a town twelve miles distant. He was pastor of three other churches besides the one at Winchester, and he preached at each one Sunday in the month. After a while he put in his appearance. He was rather small in stature, and held his head somewhat to one side and looked at you with that knowing look of the parrot. He wore a pair of trousers that had been black, but were now sleet from much wear. They lacked two inches of reaching down to the feet of his high-heeled boots. He had on a long linen duster that reached below his knees. Beneath this was a faded Prince Albert coat and a vest much too small. On his head there sat, slightly tipped, a high-topped beaver that seemed to have been hidden between two mattresses all the week and taken out and straightened for Sunday wear. In his hand he held a walking cane.

Thus clad he came toward the church, his body thrown slightly back, walking leisurely with the air of quiet dignity possessed by the man sure of his standing, and not under the necessity of asserting it overmuch in his carriage.

The brothers pulled off their hats and the sisters put on their best smiles as the parson approached. After a cordial handshake all around, the preacher entered the church to begin the services. After singing a hymn and praying, he took for his text the following "passige of scripter:"

"It air harder fur a camel to git through de eye of a cambric needle den fur a rich man to enter de kingdom of heben."

This was one of the parson's favorite texts, and the members all settled themselves back to have a good "speritual" time.

The preacher began his sermon in a somewhat quiet way, but the members knew that he would "warm up bye and bye." He pictured all rich men as trying to get into heaven, but, he asserted, they invariably found themselves with Dives. He exhorted his hearers to stick to Jesus. Here he pulled off his collar, and the sisters stirred and looked about them. A little later on, the preacher getting "warmer," pulled off his cuffs. The brethren laughed with a sort of joyous jumping up and down all the while—one crying "Gib me Jesus," another "Oh I am gwine home," and so on.

One sister who had a white lady's baby in her arms got happy and flung it entirely across the room, it falling into Mrs. Piedmont's lap, while the frenzied woman who threw the child climbed over benches, rushed into the pulpit, and swung to the preacher's neck, crying—"Glory! Glory! Glory!" In the meanwhile Belton had dropped down under one of the benches and was watching the proceedings with an eye of terror.

The sermon over and quiet restored, a collection was taken and given to the pastor. Mrs. Piedmont went forward to put some money on the table and took occasion to step to the pulpit and invite the pastor to dinner. Knowing that this meant chicken, the pastor unhesitatingly accepted the invitation, and when church was over accompanied Mrs. Piedmont and her family home.

The preacher caught hold of Belton's hand as they walked along. This mark of attention, esteemed by Belton as a signal honor, filled his little soul with joy. As he thought of the manner in which the preacher stirred up the people, the amount of the collection that had been given him, and the biscuits and chicken that now awaited him, Belton decided that he, too, would like to become a preacher.

Just before reaching home, according to a preconcerted plan, Belton and James Henry broke from the group and ran into the house. When the others appeared a little later on, these two were not to be seen. However, no question was asked and no search made. All things were ready and the parson sat down to eat, while the three girls stood about, glancing now and then at the table. The preacher was very voracious and began his meal as though he "meant business."

We can now reveal the whereabouts of Belton and James Henry. They had clambered into the loft for the purpose of watching the progress of the preacher's meal, calculating at each step how much he would probably leave. James Henry found a little hole in the loft directly over the table, and through this hole he did his spying. Belton took his position at the larger entrance hole, lying flat on his stomach. He poked his head down far enough to see the preacher, but held it in readiness to be snatched back, if the preacher's eyes seemed to be about to wander his way.

He was kept in a state of feverish excitement, on the one hand, by fear of detection, and on the other, by a desire to watch the meal. When about half of the biscuits were gone, and the preacher seemed as fresh as ever, Belton began to be afraid for his promised biscuit and piece of chicken. He crawled to James Henry and said hastily—"James, dees haf gone," and hurriedly resumed his watch. A moment later he called out in a whisper, "He's tuck anudder." Down goes Belton's head to resume his watch. Every time the preacher took another biscuit Belton called out the fact to James.

All of the chicken was at last destroyed and only one biscuit remained; and Belton's whole soul was now centered on that biscuit. In his eagerness to watch he leaned a good distance out, and when the preacher reached forth his hand to take the last one Belton was so overcome that he lost his balance and tumbled out of his hole on the floor, kicking, and crying over and over again: "I knowed I wuzunt goin' to git naren dem biscuits."

The startled preacher hastily arose from the table and gazed on the little fellow in bewilderment. As soon as it dawned upon him what the trouble was, he hastily got the remaining biscuit and gave it to Belton. He also discovered that his voracity had made enemies of the rest of the children, and he very adroitly passed a five cent piece around to each.

James Henry, forgetting his altitude and anxious not to lose his recompense, cried out loudly from the loft: "Amanda Ann you git mine fur me."

The preacher looked up but saw no one. Seeing that his request did not have the desired effect, James Henry soon tumbled down full of dust, straw and cobwebs, and came into possession of his appeasing money. The preacher laughed heartily and seemed to enjoy his experience highly.

The table was cleared, and the preacher and Mrs. Piedmont dismissed the children in order to discuss unmolested the subject which had prompted her to extend an invitation to the parson. In view of the intense dislike the teacher had conceived for Belton, she desired to know if it were not best to withdraw him from school altogether, rather than to subject him to the harsh treatment sure to come.

"Let me gib yer my advis, sistah Hannah. De greatest t'ing in de wul is edification. Ef our race ken git dat we ken git ebery t'ing else. Dat is de key. Git de key an' yer ken go in de house to go whare you please. As fur his beatin' de brat, yer musn't kick agin dat. He'll beat de brat to make him larn, and won't dat be a blessed t'ing? See dis scar on side my head? Old marse Sampson knocked me down wid a single-tree tryin' to make me stop larning, and God is so fixed it dat white folks is knocking es down ef we don't larn. Ef yer take Belton out of school yer'll be fighting 'genst de providence of God."

Being thus advised by her shepherd, Mrs. Piedmont decided to keep Belton in school. So on Monday Belton went back to his brutal teacher, and thither we follow him.

CHAPTER IV

THE TURNING OF A WORM

As to who Mr. Tiberius Gracchus Leonard was, or as to where he came from, nobody in Winchester, save himself, knew.

Immediately following the close of the Civil War, Rev. Samuel Christian, a poor but honorable retired minister of the M. E. Church, South, was the first teacher employed to instruct the colored children of the town.

He was one of those Southerners who had never believed in the morality of slavery, but regarded it as a deep rooted evil beyond human power to uproot. When the manacles fell from the hands of the Negroes he gladly accepted the task of removing the scales of ignorance from the blinded eyes of the race.

Tenderly he labored, valiantly he toiled in the midst of the mass of ignorance that came surging around him. But only one brief year was given to this saintly soul to endeavor to blast the mountains of stupidity which centuries of oppression had reared. He fell asleep.

The white men who were trustees of the colored school, were sorely puzzled as to what to do for a successor. A Negro, capable of teaching a school, was nowhere near. White young men of the South, generally, looked upon the work of teaching "niggers" with the utmost contempt; and any man who suggested the name of a white young lady of Southern birth as a teacher for the colored children was actually in danger of being shot by any member of the insulted family who could handle a pistol.

An advertisement was inserted in the *Washington Post* to the effect that a teacher was wanted. In answer to this advertisement Mr. Leonard came. He was a man above the medium height, and possessed a frame not large but compactly built. His forehead was low and narrow; while the back of his head looked exceedingly intellectual. Looking at him from the front you would involuntarily exclaim: "What an infamous scoundrel." Looking at him from the rear you would say: "There certainly is brain power in that head."

The glance of Mr. Leonard's eye was furtive, and his face was sour looking indeed. At times when he felt that no one was watching him, his whole countenance and attitude betokened the rage of despair.

Most people who looked at him felt that he carried in his bosom a dark secret. As to scholarship, he was unquestionably proficient. No white man in all the neighboring section, ranked with him intellectually. Despite the lack of all knowledge of his moral character and previous life, he was pronounced as much too good a man to fritter away his time on "niggers."

Such was the character of the man into whose hands was committed the destiny of the colored children of Winchester.

As his mother foresaw would be the case, Belton was singled out by the teacher as a special object on which he might expend his spleen. For a man to be as spiteful as he was, there must have been something gnawing at his heart. But toward Bernard none of this evil spirit was manifested. He seemed to have chosen Bernard for his pet, and Belton for his "pet aversion." To the one he was all kindness; while to the other he was cruel in the extreme.

Often he would purchase flowers from the florist and give to Bernard to bear home to his mother. On these days he would seemingly take pains to give Belton fresh bruises to take home to *his* mother. When he had a particularly good dinner he would invite Bernard to dine with him, and would be sure to find some pretext for forbidding Belton to partake of his own common meal.

Belton was by no means insensible to all these acts of discrimination. Nor did Bernard fail to perceive that he, himself, was the teacher's pet. He clambered on to the teacher's knees, played with his mustache, and often took his watch and wore it. The teacher seemed to be truly fond of him.

The children all ascribed this partiality to the color of Bernard's skin, and they all, except Belton, began to envy and despise Bernard. Of course they told their parents of the teacher's partiality and their parents thus became embittered against the teacher. But however much they might object to him and desire his removal, their united protests would not have had the weight of a feather. So the teacher remained at Winchester for twelve years. During all these years he instructed our young friends Belton and Bernard.

Strangely enough, his ardent love for Bernard and his bitter hatred of Belton accomplished the very same result in respect to their acquirements. The teacher soon discovered that both boys were talented far beyond the ordinary, and that both were ambitious. He saw that the way to wound and humiliate Belton was to make Bernard excel him. Thus he bent all of his energies to improve Bernard's mind. Whenever he heard Belton recite he brought all of his talents to bear to point out his failures, hoping thus to exalt Bernard, out of whose work he strove to keep all blemishes. Thus Belton became accustomed to the closest scrutiny, and prepared himself accordingly. The result was that Bernard did not gain an inch on him.

The teacher introduced the two boys into every needed field of knowledge, as they grew older, hoping always to find some branch in which Bernard might display unquestioned superiority. There were two studies in which the two rivals dug deep to see which could bring forth the richest treasures; and these gave coloring to the whole of their after lives. One, was the History of the United States, and the other, Rhetoric. Light but not bright,

In history, that portion that charmed them most was the story of the rebellion against the yoke of England. Far and wide they went in search of everything that would throw light on this epoch. They became immersed in the spirit of that heroic age.

As a part of their rhetorical training they were taught to declaim. Thanks to their absorption in the history of the Revolution, their minds ran to the sublime in literature; and they strove to secure pieces to declaim that recited the most heroic deeds of man, of whatever nationality.

Leonidas, Marco Bozarris, Arnold Winklereid, Louis Kossuth, Robert Emmett, Martin Luther, Patrick Henry and such characters furnished the pieces almost invariably declaimed. They threw their whole souls into these, and the only natural thing resulted. No human soul can breathe the atmosphere of heroes and read with bated breath their deeds of daring without craving for the opportunity to do the like. Thus the education of these two young men went on.

At the expiration of twelve years they had acquired an academic education that could not be surpassed anywhere in the land. Their reputation as brilliant students and eloquent speakers had spread over the whole surrounding country.

The teacher decided to graduate the young men; and he thought to utilize the occasion as a lasting humiliation of Belton and exaltation of his favorite, Bernard Belgrave. Belton felt this.

In the first part of this last school year of the boys, he had told them to prepare for a grand commencement exercise, and they acted accordingly. Each one chose his subject and began the preparation of his oration early in the session, each keeping his subject and treatment secret from the other.

The teacher had announced that numerous white citizens would be present; among them the congressman from the district and the mayor of the town. Belton determined upon two things, away down in his soul. He determined to win in the oratorical contest, and to get his revenge on his teacher on the day that the teacher had planned for his—(Belton's) humiliation. Bernard did not have the incentive that Belton did; but defeat was ever galling to him, and he, too, had determined to win.

The teacher often reviewed the progress made by Bernard on his oration, but did not notice Belton's at all. He strove to make Bernard's oration as nearly perfect as labor and skill could make it. But Belton was not asleep as to either of the resolutions he had formed. Some nights he could be seen stealing away from the congressman's residence. On others he could be seen leaving the neighborhood of the school, with a spade in one hand and a few carpenter's tools in the other.

He went to the congressman, who was a polished orator with a national reputation, in order that he might purge his oration from its impurities of speech. As the congressman read the oration and perceived the depth of thought, the logical arrangement, the beauty and rhythm of language, and the wide research displayed, he opened his eyes wide with astonishment. He was amazed that a young man of such uncommon talents could have grown up in his town and he not know it. Belton's marvelous talents won his respect and admiration, and he gave him access to his library and criticized his oration whenever needed.

Secretly and silently preparations went on for the grand conflict. At last the day came. The colored men and women of the place laid aside all work to attend the exercises. The forward section of seats was reserved for the white people. The congressman, the mayor, the school trustees and various other men of standing came, accompanied by their wives and daughters.

Scholars of various grades had parts to perform on the programme, but the eyes of all sought the bottom of the page where were printed the names of the two oratorical gladiators:

"BELTON PIEDMONT.
BERNARD BELGRAVE."

The teacher had given Bernard the last place, deeming that the more advantageous. He appointed the congressman, the mayor, and one of the school trustees to act as judges, to decide to whom he should award a beautiful gold medal for the more excellent oration. The congressman politely declined and named another trustee in his stead. Then the contest began. As Belton walked up on the platform the children greeted him with applause. He announced as his subject: "The Contribution of the Anglo-Saxon to the Cause of Human Liberty." In his strong, earnest voice, he began to roll off his well turned periods. The whole audience seemed as if in a trance. His words made their hearts burn, and time and again he made them burst forth in applause.

The white people who sat and listened to his speech looked upon it as a very revelation to them, they themselves not having had as clear a conception of the glory of their race as this Negro now revealed. When he had finished, white men and women crowded to the front to congratulate him upon his effort, and it was many minutes before quiet was restored sufficiently to allow the programme to proceed.

Bernard took his position on the platform, announcing as his subject: "Robert Emmett." His voice was sweet and well modulated and never failed to charm. Admiration was plainly depicted on every face as he proceeded. He brought to bear all the graces of a polished orator, and more than once tears came into the eyes of his listeners. Particularly affecting was his description of Emmett's death. At the conclusion it was evident that his audience felt that it would have been difficult to have handled that subject better.

The judges now retired to deliberate as to whom to give the prize. While they are out, let us examine Belton's plans for carrying out the second thing, upon the accomplishment of which he was determined; viz., revenge.

In the rear of the schoolhouse, there stood an old wood-shed. For some slight offence the teacher had, two or three years back, made Belton the fire-maker for the balance of his school life instead of passing the task around according to custom. Thus the care of the woodhouse had fallen permanently to Belton's lot.

During the last year Belton had dug a large hole running from the floor of the wood-shed to a point under the platform of the school room. The dirt from this underground channel he cast into a deep old unused well, not far distant. Once under the platform, he kept on digging, making the hole larger by far. Numerous rocks abounded in the neighborhood, and these he used to wall up his underground room, so that it would hold water. Just in the middle of the school-room platform he cut, from beneath, a square hole, taking in the spot where the teacher invariably stood when addressing the school. He cut the boards until they lacked but a very little, indeed, of being cut through. All looked well above, but a baby would not be safe standing thereon. Belton contrived a kind of prop with a weight attached. This prop would serve to keep the cut section from breaking through. The attached weight was at rest in a hole left in the wall of the cavity near its top. If you dislocated the weight, the momentum that it would gather in the fall would pull down the prop to which it was attached.

Finally, Belton fastened a strong rope to the weight, and ran the rope under the schoolhouse floor until it was immediately beneath his seat. With an auger he made a hole in the floor and brought the end through. He managed to keep this bit of rope concealed, while at the same time he had perfect command of his trap door.

For two or three nights previous to commencement day Belton had worked until nearly morning filling this cistern with water. Now when through delivering his oration, he had returned to his seat to await the proper moment for the payment of his teacher. The judges were out debating the question as to who had won. They seemed to be unable to decide who was victorious and beckoned for the teacher to step outside.

They said: "That black nigger has beat the yellow one all to pieces this time, but we don't like to see nigger blood triumph over any Anglo-Saxon blood. Ain't there any loop-hole where we can give it to Bernard, anyhow?"

"Well, yes," said the teacher eagerly, "on the ground of good behavior."

"There you hit it," said the Mayor. "So we all decide."

The judges filed in, and the Mayor arose to announce their decision. "We award," said he to the breathless audience, "the prize to Bernard Belgrave."

"No! no! no!" burst forth from persons all over the house. The congressman arose and went up to Belton and congratulated him upon his triumph over oratory, and lamented his defeat by prejudice. This action caused a perceptible stir in the entire audience.

The teacher went to his desk and produced a large gold medal. He took his accustomed place on the platform and began thus:

"Ladies and Gentlemen, this is the proudest moment of my life." He got no further. Belton had pulled the rope, the rope had caused the weight to fall, and the weight had pulled the prop and down had gone the teacher into a well of water.

"Murder! Murder! Murder!" he cried "Help! Help! Help! I am drowning. Take me out, it is cold."

The audience rushed forward expecting to find the teacher in a

dangerous situation; but they found him standing, apparently un-
harmed, in a cistern, the water being a little more than waist deep.
Their fright gave way to humor and a merry shout went up from
the throats of the scholars.

The colored men and women laughed to one side, while the
white people smiled as though they had admired the feat as a fine
specimen of falling from the sublime to the ridiculous. Bending
down over the well, the larger students caught hold of the teacher's
arms and lifted him out.

He stood before the audience wet and shivering, his clothes sticking to him, and water dripping from his hair. The medal was gone.
The teacher dismissed the audience, drew his last month's pay and
left that night for parts unknown.

Sometimes, even a worm will turn when trodden upon.

CHAPTER V

BELTON FINDS A FRIEND

Long before the rifle ball, the cannon shot, and the exploding shell were through their fiendish task of covering the earth with mortals slain; while the startled air was yet busy in hurrying to Heaven the groans of the dying soldier, accompanied as they were by the despairing shrieks of his loved ones behind; while horrid War, in frenzied joy, yet waved his bloody sword over the nation's head, and sought with eager eagle eyes every drop of clotted gore over which he might exult; in the midst of such direful days as these, there were those at the North whom the love of God and the eye of faith taught to leap over the scene of strife to prepare the trembling negro for the day of freedom, which, refusing to have a dawn, had burst in meridian splendor upon his dazzled gaze.

Into the southland there came rushing consecrated Christians, men and women, eager to provide for the negro a Christian education. Those who stayed behind gathered up hoarded treasures and gladly poured them into the lap of the South for the same laudable purpose. As a result of the coming of this army of workers, bearing in their arms millions of money, ere many years had sped, well nigh every southern state could proudly boast of one or more colleges where the aspiring negro might quench his thirst for knowledge.

So when Bernard and Belton had finished their careers at the Winchester public school, colleges abounded in the South beckoning them to enter. Bernard preferred to go to a northern institution, and his mother sent him to enter Harvard University.

Belton was poor and had no means of his own with which to pursue his education; but by the hand of providence a most unexpected door was opened to him. The Winchester correspondent of the *Richmond Daily Temps* reported the commencement exercises of the Winchester public school of the day that Belton graduated. The congressman present at the exercises spoke so highly of Belton's speech that the correspondent secured a copy from Belton and sent it to the editor of *The Temps*.

This was printed in *The Temps* and created a great sensation in political and literary circles in every section of the country. Every newspaper of any consequence reproduced the oration in full. It was published and commented upon by the leading journals of England. The President of the United States wrote a letter of congratulation to Belton. Everywhere the piece was hailed as a classic.

After reading the oration, Mr. V. M. King, editor of *The Temps,* decided to take it home with him and read it to his wife. She met him at the door and as he kissed her she noticed that there was a sober look in his eye. Tenderly he brushed back a few stray locks of his wife's hair, saying as he did so, in a somewhat troubled tone: "Wife, it has come at last. May the good Lord cease not to watch over our beloved but erring land." She inquired as to what he meant. He led her to his study and read to her Belton's oration.

In order to understand the words which we have just quoted as being spoken by him to his wife, let us, while he reads, become a little better acquainted with Mr. King and his paper, *The Temps.*

Mr. King was born and reared in Virginia, was educated at a Northern University, and had sojourned for several years in England. He was a man of the broadest culture. For several years he had given the negro problem most profound study. His views on the subject were regarded by the white people of the South as ultraliberal. These views he exploited through his paper, *The Temps,* with a boldness and vigor, gaining thereby great notoriety.

Though a democrat in politics, he was most bitterly opposed to the practice, almost universal in the South, of cheating the negro out of his right to vote. He preached that it was unjust to the negro and fatal to the morals of the whites.

On every possible occasion he viciously assaulted the practice of lynching, denouncing it in most scathing terms. In short, he was an outspoken advocate of giving the negro every right accorded him by the Constitution of the United States.

He saw the South leading the young negro boy and girl to school, where, at the expense of the state, they were taught to read history and learn what real liberty was, and the glorious struggles through which the human race had come in order to possess it. He foresaw that the rising, educated negro would allow his eye to linger long on this bloody but glorious page until that most contagious of diseases, devotion to liberty, infected his soul.

He reasoned that the negro who had endured the hardships of slavery might spend his time looking back and thanking God for that from which he had made his escape; but the young negro, knowing nothing of physical slavery, would be peering into the future, measuring the distance that he had yet to go before he was truly free, and would be asking God and his own right arm for the power to secure whatever rights were still withheld.

He argued that, living as the negro did beneath the American flag, known as the flag of freedom, studying American history, and listening on the outer edge of great Fourth of July crowds to eloquent orators discourse on freedom, it was only a matter of a few years before the negro would deify liberty as the Anglo-Saxon race had done, and count it a joy to perish on her altar.

In order that the Republic might ever stand, he knew that the principles of liberty would have to be continually taught with all the eloquence and astuteness at command; and if this teaching had the desired effect upon the white man it would also be powerful enough to awaken the negro standing by his side.

So, his ear was to the ground, expecting every moment to hear the far off sounds of awakened negroes coming to ask for liberty, and if refused, to slay or be slain.

When he read Belton's oration he saw that the flame of liberty was in his heart, her sword in his hand, and the disdain of death stamped on his brow. He felt that Belton was the morning star which told by its presence that dawn was near at hand.

Thus it was that he said to his wife: "Wife, it has come at last. May the good Lord cease not to watch over our beloved land."

This expression was not the offspring of fear as to the outcome of a possible conflict, for, Anglo-Saxon like, that was with him a foregone conclusion in favor of his own race. But he shuddered at the awful carnage that would of necessity ensue if two races, living house to house, street to street, should be equally determined upon a question at issue, equally disdainful of life, fighting with the rancor always attendant upon a struggle between two races that mutually despise and detest each other.

He knew that it was more humane, more in accordance with right, more acceptable with God, to admit to the negro that Anglo-Saxon doctrine of the equality of man was true, rather than to murder the negro for accepting him at his word, though spoken to others.

Feeling thus, he pleaded with his people to grant to the negro his rights, though he never hinted at a possible rebellion, for fear that the mention of it might hasten the birth of the idea in the brain of the negro.

That evening, after he had read the oration to his wife and told her of his forebodings, he sat with his face buried in his hands, brooding over the situation. Late in the night he retired to rest, and the next morning, when he awoke, his wife was standing by his bed, calling him. She saw that his sleep was restless and thought that he was having troubled dreams. And so he was.

He dreamed that a large drove of fatted swine were munching acorns in a very dense forest of oaks, both tall and large. The oaks were sending the acorns down in showers, and the hogs were greedily consuming them. The hogs ate so many that they burst open, and from their rotting carcasses fresh oaks sprang and grew with surprising rapidity. A dark cloud arose and a terrible hurricane swept over the forest; and the old and new oaks fought furiously in the storm, until a loud voice, like unto that of a God, cried out above all the din of the hurricane, saying in tones of thunder: "Know ye not that ye are parents and children? Parents, recognize your children. Children, be proud of the parents from whom you spring."

The hurricane ceased, the clouds sped away as if in terror, and the oaks grew up together under a clear sky of the purest blue, and beautiful birds of all kinds built their nests in the trees, and carolled forth the sweetest songs.

He placed upon the dream the following interpretation:

The swine were the negroes. The oak trees were the white people. The acorns were the doctrine of human liberty, everywhere preached by Anglo-Saxons. The negroes, feasting off of the same thought, had become the same kind of being as the white man, and grew up to a point of equality. The hurricane was the contest between the two races over the question of equality. The voice was intended to inform the whites that they had brought about these aspirations in the bosom of the negro, and that the liberty-loving negro was their legitimate offspring, and not a bastard. The whites should recognize their own doings. On the other hand, the negro should not be over boastful, and should recognize that the lofty conception of the dignity of man and value and true character of liberty were taught him by the Anglo-Saxon. The birds betokened a happy adjustment of all differences; and the dream that began in the gloom of night ended in the dawn of day.

Mr. King was very cheerful, therefore, and decided to send to Winchester for Belton, thinking that it might be a wise thing to keep an eye and a friendly hand on a young negro of such promise. In the course of a couple of days, Belton, in response to his request, arrived in Richmond. He called at the office of *The Temps* and was ushered into Mr. King's office.

Mr. King had him take a seat. He enquired of Belton his history, training, etc. He also asked as to his plans for the future. Finding that Belton was desirous of securing a college education, but was destitute of funds, Mr. King gladly embraced the opportunity of displaying his kind interest. He offered to pay Belton's way through college, and the offer was gladly accepted.

He told Belton to call at his home that evening at seven o'clock to receive a check for his entire college course. At the appointed hour Belton appeared at Mr. King's residence.

Mr. King was sitting on his front porch, between his wife and aged mother, while his two children, a girl and boy, were playing on the lawn. Belton was invited to take a seat, much to his surprise.

Seeing a stranger, the children left their play and came to their father, one on each side. They looked with questioning eyes from father to Belton, as if seeking to know the purpose of the visit.

Mr. King took the check from his pocket and extended it toward Belton, and said: "Mr. Piedmont, this will carry you through college. I have only one favor to ask of you. In all your dealings with my people recognize the fact that there are two widely separated classes of us, and that there is a good side to the character of the worst class. Always seek for and appeal to that side of their nature."

Belton very feelingly thanked Mr. King, and assured him that he would treasure his words. He was true to his promise, and decided from that moment to never class all white men together, whatever might be the provocation, and to never regard any class as totally depraved.

This is one of the keys to his future life. Remember it.

CHAPTER VI

A Young Rebel

In the city of Nashville, Tennessee, there is a far famed institution of learning called Stowe University, in honor of Mrs. Harriet Beecher Stowe, author of "Uncle Tom's Cabin."

This institution was one of the many scores of its kind, established in the South by Northern philanthropy, for the higher education of the Negro. Though called a university, it was scarcely more than a normal school with a college department attached.

It was situated just on the outskirts of the city, on a beautiful ten-acre plot of ground. The buildings were five in number, consisting of a dormitory for young men, two for young ladies, a building for recitations, and another, called the teachers' mansion; for the teachers resided there. These buildings were very handsome, and were so arranged upon the level campus as to present a very attractive sight.

With the money which had been so generously given him by Mr. King, Belton entered this school. That was a proud day in his life when he stepped out of the carriage and opened the University gate, feeling that he, a Negro, was privileged to enter college. Julius Cæsar, on entering Rome in triumph, with the world securely chained to his chariot wheels; Napoleon, bowing to receive the diadem of the Cæsars' won by the most notable victories ever known to earth; General Grant, on his triumphal tour around the globe, when kings and queens were eager rivals to secure from this man of humble birth the sweeter smile; none of these were more full of pleasurable emotion than this poor Negro lad, who now with elastic step and beating heart marched with head erect beneath the arch of the doorway leading into Stowe University.

Belton arrived on the Saturday preceding the Monday on which school would open for that session. He found about three hundred and sixty students there from all parts of the South, the young women outnumbering the young men in about the proportion of two to one.

On the Sunday night following his arrival the students all assembled in the general assembly room of the recitation building, which room, in the absence of a chapel, was used as the place for religious worship. The president of the school, a venerable white minister from the North, had charge of the service that evening. He did not on this occasion preach a sermon, but devoted the hour to discoursing upon the philanthropic work done by the white people of the North for the freedmen of the South.

A map of the United States was hanging on the wall, facing the assembled school. On this map there were black dots indicating all places where a school of learning had been planted for the colored people by their white friends of the North. Belton sat closely scrutinizing the map. His eyes swept from one end to the other. Persons were allowed to ask any questions desired, and Belton was very inquisitive.

When the hour of the lecture was over he was deeply impressed with three thoughts: First, his heart went out in love to those who had given so freely of their means and to those who had dedicated their lives to the work of uplifting his people.

Secondly, he saw an immense army of young men and women being trained in the very best manner in every section of the South, to go forth to grapple with the great problems before them. He felt proud of being a member of so promising an army, and felt that they were to determine the future of the race. In fact, this thought was reiterated time and again by the president.

Thirdly, Belton was impressed that it was the duty of those receiving such great blessings to accomplish achievements worthy of the care bestowed. He felt that the eyes of the North and of the civilized world were upon them to see the fruits of the great labor and money spent upon them.

Before he retired to rest that night, he besought God to enable him and his people, as a mark of appreciation of what had been done for the race, to rise to the full measure of just expectation and prove worthy of all the care bestowed. He went through school, therefore, as though the eyes of the world were looking at the race enquiringly; the eyes of the North expectantly; and the eyes of God lovingly,—three grand incentives to his soul.

When these schools were first projected, the White South that then was, fought them with every weapon at its command. Ridicule, villification, ostracism, violence, arson, murder were all employed to hinder the progress of the work. Outsiders looked on and thought it strange that they should do this. But, just as a snake, though a venomous animal, by instinct knows its enemy and fights for its life with desperation, just so the Old South instinctively foresaw danger to its social fabric as then constituted, and therefore despised and fought the agencies that were training and inspiring the future leaders of the Negro race in such a manner as to render a conflict inevitable and of doubtful termination.

The errors in the South, anxious for eternal life, rightfully feared these schools more than they would have feared factories making powder, moulding balls and fashioning cannons. But the New South, the South that, in the providence of God, is yet to be, could not have been formed in the womb of time had it not been for these schools. And so the receding murmurs of the scowling South that was, are lost in the gladsome shouts of the South which, please God, is yet to be.

But lest we linger too long, let us enter school here with Belton. On the Monday following the Sunday night previously indicated, Belton walked into the general assembly room to take his seat with the other three hundred and sixty pupils. It was the custom for the school to thus assemble for devotional exercises. The teachers sat in a row across the platform, facing the pupils. The president sat immediately in front of the desk, in the center of the platform, and the teachers sat on either side of him.

To Belton's surprise, he saw a colored man sitting on the right side of and next to the president. He was sitting there calmly, self-possessed, exactly like the rest. He crossed his legs and stroked his beard in a most matter of fact way. Belton stared at this colored man, with his lips apart and his body bent forward. He let his eyes scan the faces of all the white teachers, male and female, but would end up with a stare at the colored man sitting there. Finally, he hunched his seat-mate with his elbow and asked what man that was. He was told that it was the colored teacher of the faculty.

Belton knew that there was a colored teacher in the school but he had no idea that he would be thus honored with a seat with the rest of the teachers. A broad, happy smile spread over his face, and his eyes danced with delight. He had, in his boyish heart, dreamed of the equality of the races and sighed and hoped for it; but here, he beheld it in reality. Though he, as a rule, shut his eyes when prayer was being offered, he kept them open that morning, and peeped through his fingers at that thrilling sight,—a colored man on equal terms with the white college professors.

Just before the classes were dismissed to their respective class rooms, the teachers came together in a group to discuss some matter, in an informal way. The colored teacher was in the center of the group and discussed the matter as freely as any; and he was listened to with every mark of respect. Belton kept a keen watch on the conference and began rubbing his hands and chuckling to himself with delight at seeing the colored teacher participating on equal terms with the other teachers.

The colored teacher's views seemed about to prevail, and as one after another the teachers seemed to fall in line with him Belton could not contain himself longer, but clapped his hands and gave a loud, joyful, "Ha! ha!"

The eyes of the whole school were on him in an instant, and the faculty turned around to discover the source and cause of the disorder. But Belton had come to himself as soon as he made the noise, and in a twinkling was as quiet and solemn looking as a mouse.

The faculty resumed its conference and the students passed the query around as to what was the matter with the "newcomer." A number tapped their heads significantly, saying: "Wrong here." How far wrong were they! They should have put their hands over their hearts and said: "The fire of patriotism here;" for Belton had here on a small scale, the gratification of the deepest passion of his soul, viz., Equality of the races. And what pleased him as much as anything else was the dignified, matter of fact way in which the teacher bore his honors. Belton afterwards discovered that this colored man was vice-president of the faculty.

On a morning, later in the session, the president announced that the faculty would hold its regular weekly meeting that evening, but that he would have to be in the city to attend to other matters. Belton's heart bounded at the announcement. Knowing that the colored teacher was vice-president of the faculty, he saw that he would preside. Belton determined to see that meeting of the faculty if it cost him no end of trouble. He could not afford, under any circumstances, to fail to see that colored man preside over those white men and women.

That night, about 8:30 o'clock, when the faculty meeting had progressed about half way, Belton made a rope of his bed clothes and let himself down to the ground from the window of his room on the second floor of the building. About twenty yards distant was the "mansion," in one room of which the teachers held their faculty meetings. The room in which the meeting was held was on the side of the "mansion" furthest from the dormitory from which Belton had just come. The "mansion" dog was Belton's friend, and a soft whistle quieted his bark. Belton stole around to the side of the house, where the meeting was being held. The weather was mild and the window was hoisted. Belton fell on his knees and crawled to the window, and pulling it up cautiously peeped in. He saw the colored teacher in the chair in the center of the room and others sitting about here and there. He gazed with rapture on the sight. He watched, unmolested, for a long while.

One of the lady teachers was tearing up a piece of paper and arose to come to the window to throw it out. Belton was listening, just at that time, to what the colored teacher was saying, and did not see the lady coming in his direction. Nor did the lady see the form of a man until she was near at hand. At the sight she threw up her hands and screamed loudly from fright. Belton turned and fled precipitately. The chicken-coop door had been accidentally left open and Belton, unthinkingly, jumped into the chicken house. The chickens set up a lively cackle, much to his chagrin. He grasped an old rooster to stop him, but missing the rooster's throat, the rooster gave the alarm all the more vociferously. Teachers had now crowded to the window and were peering out. Some of the men started to the door to come out. Belton saw this movement and decided that the best way for him to do was to play chicken thief and run. Grasping a hen with his other hand, he darted out of the chicken house and fled from the college ground, the chickens squalling all the while. He leapt the college fence at a bound and wrung off the heads of the chickens to stop the noise.

The teachers decided that they had been visited by a Negro, hunting for chickens; laughed heartily at their fright and resumed deliberations. Thus again a patriot was mistaken for a chicken thief; and in the South to-day a race that dreams of freedom, equality, and empire, far more than is imagined, is put down as a race of chicken thieves. As in Belton's case, this conception diverts attention from places where startling things would otherwise be discovered.

In due time Belton crept back to the dormitory, and by a signal agreed upon, roused his room-mate, who let down the rope, by means of which he ascended; and when seated gave his room-mate an account of his adventure.

Sometime later on, Belton in company with another student was sent over to a sister University in Nashville to carry a note for the president. This University also had a colored teacher who was one point in advance of Belton's. This teacher ate at the same table with the white teachers, while Belton's teacher ate with the students. Belton passed by the dining room of the teachers of this sister University and saw the colored teacher enjoying a meal with the white teachers. He could not enjoy the sight as much as he would have liked, from thinking about the treatment his teacher was receiving. He had not, prior to this, thought of that discrimination, but now it burned him.

He returned to his school and before many days had passed he had called together all the male students. He informed them that they ought to perfect a secret organization and have a password. They all agreed to secrecy and Belton gave this as the password: "Equality or Death."

He then told them that it was his ambition and purpose to coerce the white teachers into allowing the colored teacher to eat with them. They all very readily agreed; for the matter of his eating had been thoroughly canvassed for a number of sessions, but it seemed as though no one dared to suggest a combination. During slavery all combinations of slaves were sedulously guarded against, and a fear of combinations seems to have been injected into the Negro's very blood.

The very boldness of Belton's idea swept the students away from the lethargic harbor in which they had been anchored, and they were eager for action. Belton was instructed to prepare the complaint, which they all agreed to sign. They decided that it was to be presented to the president just before devotional exercises and an answer was to be demanded forthwith. One of the young men had a sister among the young lady students, and, through her Belton's rebellion was organized among the girls and their signatures secured.

The eventful morning came. The teachers glanced over the assembled students, and were surprised to see them dressed in their best clothes as though it was the Sabbath. There was a quiet satisfied look on their faces that the teachers did not understand.

The president arrived a little late and found an official envelope on his desk. He hurriedly broke the seal and began to read. His color came and went. The teachers looked at him wonderingly. The president laid the document aside and began the devotional exercises. He was nervous throughout, and made several blunders. He held his hymn book upside down while they were singing, much to the amusement of the school. It took him some time to find the passage of scripture which he desired to read, and after reading forgot for some seconds to call on some one to pray.

When the exercises were through he arose and took the document nervously in hand. He said; "I have in my hands a paper from the students of this institution concerning a matter with which they have nothing to do. This is my answer. The classes will please retire." Here he gave three strokes to the gong, the signal for dispersion. But not a student moved. The president was amazed. He could not believe his own eyes. He rang the gong a second time and yet no one moved. He then in nervous tones repeated his former assertions and then pulled the gong nervously many times in succession. All remained still. At a signal from Belton, all the students lifted their right hands, each bearing a small white board on which was printed in clear type: "Equality or Death."

The president fell back, aghast, and the white teachers were all struck dumb with fear. They had not dreamed that a combination of their pupils was possible, and they knew not what it foreboded. A number grasped the paper that was giving so much trouble and read it. They all then held a hurried consultation and assured the students that the matter should receive due attention.

The president then rang the gong again but the students yet remained. Belton then arose and stated that it was the determination of the students to not move an inch unless the matter was adjusted then and there. And that faculty of white teachers beat a hasty retreat and held up the white flag! They agreed that the colored teacher should eat with them.

The students broke forth into cheering, and flaunted a black flag on which was painted in white letters; "Victory." They rose and marched out of doors two by two, singing "John Brown's Body lies mouldering in the grave, and we go marching on."

The confused and bewidered teachers remained behind, busy with their thoughts. They felt like hens who had lost their broods. The cringing, fawning, sniffling, cowardly Negro which slavery left, had disappeared, and a new Negro, self-respecting, fearless, and determined in the assertion of his rights was at hand.

Ye who chronicle history and mark epochs in the career of races and nations must put here a towering, gigantic, century stone, as marking the passing of one and the ushering in of another great era in the history of the colored people of the United States. Rebellions, for one cause or another, broke out in almost every one of these schools presided over by white faculties, and as a rule, the Negro students triumphed.

These men who engineered and participated in these rebellions were the future leaders of their race. In these rebellions, they learned the power of combinations, and that white men could be made to capitulate to colored men under certain circumstances. In these schools, probably one hundred thousand students had these thoughts instilled in them. These one hundred thousand went to their respective homes and told of their prowess to their playmates who could not follow them to the college walls. In the light of these facts the great events yet to be recorded are fully accounted for.

Remember that this was Belton's first taste of rebellion against the whites for the securing of rights denied simply because of color. In after life he is the moving, controlling, guiding spirit in one on a far larger scale; it need not come as a surprise. His teachers and school-mates predicted this of him.

CHAPTER VII

A Sermon, a Sock and a Fight

Belton remained at Stowe University, acquiring fame as an orator and scholar. His intellect was pronounced by all to be marvelously bright.

We now pass over all his school career until we come to the closing days of the session in which he graduated. School was to close on Thursday, and the Sunday night previous had been designated as the time for the Baccalaureate sermon. On this occasion the entire school assembled in the general assembly room,—the graduating class occupying the row of front seats stretching across the room. The class, this year, numbered twenty-five; and they presented an appearance that caused the hearts of the people to swell with pride.

Dr. Lovejoy, president of the University, was to preach the sermon. He chose for his text, "The Kingdom of God is within us." We shall choose from his discourse just such thoughts as may throw light upon some events yet to be recorded, which might not otherwise be accounted for:

"Young men, we shall soon push you forth into the midst of a turbulent world, to play such a part as the voice of God may assign you. You go forth, amid the shouts and huzzahs of cheering friends, and the anxious prayers of the faithful of God. The part that you play, the character of your return journey, triumphant or inglorious, will depend largely upon how well you have learned the lesson of this text. Remember that the kingdom of God is within you. Do not go forth into the world to demand favors of the world, but go forth to give unto the world. Be strong in your own hearts.

"The world is like unto a wounded animal that has run a long way and now lies stretched upon the ground, the blood oozing forth from gaping wounds and pains darting through its entire frame. The huntsman, who comes along to secure and drink the feverish milk of this animal that is all but a rotting carcass, seriously endangers his own well being. So, young men, do not look upon this dying, decaying world to feed and support you. You must feed and support it. Carry fresh, warm, invigorating blood in your veins to inject into the veins of the world. This is far safer and nobler than sticking the lance into the swollen veins of the world, to draw forth its putrid blood for your own use. I not only exhort you but I warn you. You may go to this dying animal as a surgeon, and proceed to cut off the sound portions for your own use. You may deceive the world for awhile, but it will, ere long, discover whether you are a vandal or a surgeon; and if it finds you to be the former, when you are closest to its bosom, it will squeeze you tightly and tear your face to shreds.

"I wish now to apply these thoughts to your immediate circumstances.

"You shall be called upon to play a part in the adjusting of positions between the negro and Anglo-Saxon races of the South. The present status of affairs cannot possibly remain. The Anglo-Saxon race must surrender some of its outposts, and the negro will occupy these. To bring about this evacuation on the part of the Anglo-

Saxon, and the forward march of the negro, will be your task. This is a grave and delicate task, fraught with much good or evil, weal or woe. Let us urge you to undertake it in the spirit to benefit the world, and not merely to advance your own glory.

"The passions of men will soon be running high, and by feeding these passions with the food for which they clamor you may attain the designation of a hero. But, with all the energy of my soul, I exhort you to not play with fire, merely for the sake of the glare that it may cast upon you. Use no crisis for self-aggrandizement. Be so full of your own soul's wealth that these temptations may not appeal to you. When your vessel is ploughing the roughest seas and encountering the fiercest gales, consult as your chart the welfare of the ship and crew, though you may temporarily lose fame as a captain.

"Young men, you are highly favored of God. A glorious destiny awaits your people. The gates of the beautiful land of the future are flung wide. Your people stand before these gates peering eagerly within. They are ready to march. They are waiting for their commanders and the command to move forward. You are the commanders who must give the command. I urge, I exhort, I beseech you, my dear boys, to think not of yourselves. Let your kingdom be within. Lead them as they ought to be led, taking no thought to your own glory.

"If you heed my voice you shall become true patriots. If you disregard it, you will become time-serving demagogues, playing upon the passions of the people for the sake of short-lived notoriety. Such men would corral all the tigers in the forest and organize them into marauding regiments simply for the honor of being in the lead. Be ye none of these, my boys. May your Alma Mater never feel called upon to cry to God in anguish to paralyze the hand that she herself has trained.

"Be not a burrowing parasite, feasting off of the world's raw blood. Let the world draw life from you. Use not the misfortunes of your people as stones of a monument erected to your name. If you do, the iron fist of time will knock it over on your grave to crumble your decaying bones to further dust.

"Always serve the world as the voice of good conscience, instructed by a righteous God, may direct. Do this and thou shalt live; live in the sweetened memory of your countrymen; live in the heart of your Alma Mater; live when the earth is floating dust, when the stars are dead, when the sun is a charred and blackened ruin; live on the bosom of your Savior, by the throne of his God, in the eternal Heavens."

The teacher's soul was truly in his discourse and his thoughts sank deep into the hearts of his hearers. None listened more attentively than Belton. None were more deeply impressed than he. None more readily incorporated the principles enumerated as a part of their living lives.

When the preacher sat down he bowed his head in his hands. His frame shook. His white locks fluttered in the gentle spring breeze. In silence he prayed. He earnestly implored God to not allow his work and words to be in vain. The same fervent prayer was on Belton's lips, rising from the center of his soul. Somewhere, these prayers met, locked arms and went before God together. In due time the answer came.

This sermon had much to do with Belton's subsequent career. But an incident apparently trivial in itself was the occasion of a private discourse that had even greater influence over him. It occurred on Thursday following the night of the delivery of the sermon just reported. It was on this wise:

Belton had, in everything, excelled his entire class, and was, according to the custom, made valedictorian. His room-mate was insanely jealous of him, and sought every way possible to humiliate him. He had racked his brain for a scheme to play on Belton on commencement day, and he at last found one that gave him satisfaction.

There was a student in Stowe University who was noted for his immense height and for the size and scent of his feet. His feet perspired freely, summer and winter, and the smell was exceedingly offensive. On this account he roomed to himself. Whenever other students called to see him he had a very effective way of getting rid of them, when he judged that they had stayed long enough. He would complain of a corn and forthwith pull off a shoe. If his room was crowded, this act invariably caused it to be empty. The fame of these feet spread to the teachers and young ladies, and, in fact, to the city. And the huge Mississippian seemed to relish the distinction.

Whenever Belton was to deliver an oration he always arranged his clothes the night beforehand. So, on the Wednesday night of the week in question, he carefully brushed and arranged his clothes for the next day. In the valedictory there were many really touching things, and in rehearsing it before his room-mate Belton had often shed tears. Fearing that he might be so touched that tears would come to his eyes in the final delivery, he had bought a most beautiful and costly silk handkerchief. He carefully stowed this away in the tail pocket of his handsome Prince Albert suit of lovely black. He hung his coat in the wardrobe, very carefully, so that he would merely have to take it down and put it on the next day.

His room-mate watched his movements closely, but slyly. He arose when he saw Belton hang his coat up. He went down the corridor until he arrived at the room occupied by the Mississippian. He knocked, and after some little delay, was allowed to enter.

The Mississippian was busy rehearsing his oration and did not care to be bothered. But he sat down to entertain Belton's room-mate for a while. He did not care to rehearse his oration before him and he felt able to rout him at any time. They conversed on various things for a while, when Belton's room-mate took up a book and soon appeared absorbed in reading. He was sitting on one side of a study table in the center of the room while the Mississippian was on the other. Thinking that his visitor had now stayed about long enough, the Mississippian stooped down quietly and removed one shoe. He slyly watched Belton's room-mate, chuckling inwardly. But his fun died away into a feeling of surprise when he saw that his shoeless foot was not even attracting attention.

He stooped down and pulled off the other shoe, and his surprise developed into amazement when he saw that the combined attack produced no result. Belton's room-mate seemed absorbed in reading.

The Mississippian next pulled off his coat and pretending to yawn and stretch, lifted his arms just so that the junction of his arm with his shoulder was on a direct line with his visitor's nose. Belton's room-mate made a slight grimace, but kept on reading. The Mississippian was dumbfounded.

He then signified his intention of retiring to bed and undressed, eyeing his visitor all the while, hoping that the scent of his whole body would succeed.

He got into bed and was soon snoring loudly enough to be heard two or three rooms away; but Belton's room-mate seemed to pay no attention to the snoring.

The Mississippian gave up the battle in disgust, saying to himself: "That fellow regards scents and noises just as though he was a buzzard, hatched in a cleft of the roaring Niagara Falls." So saying, he fell asleep in reality and the snoring increased in volume and speed.

Belton's room-mate now took a pair of large new socks out of his pocket and put them into the Mississippian's shoes, from which he took the dirty socks already there. Having these dirty socks, he quietly tips out of the room and returns to his and Belton's room.

Belton desired to make the speech of his life the next day, and had retired to rest early so as to be in prime nervous condition for the effort. His room-mate stole to the wardrobe and stealthily extracted the silk handkerchief and put these dirty socks in its stead.

Belton was then asleep, perhaps dreaming of the glories of the morrow.

Thursday dawned and Belton arose, fresh and vigorous. He was cheerful and buoyant that day; he was to graduate bedecked with all the honors of his class. Mr. King, his benefactor, was to be present. His mother had saved up her scant earnings and had come to see her son wind up the career on which she had sent him forth, years ago.

The assembly room was decorated with choice flowers and presented the appearance of the Garden of Eden. On one side of the room sat the young lady pupils, while on the other the young men sat. Visitors from the city came in droves and men of distinction sat on the platform. The programme was a good one, but all eyes dropped to the bottom in quest of Belton's name; for his fame as an orator was great, indeed.

The programme passed off as arranged, giving satisfaction and whetting the appetite for Belton's oration. The president announced Belton's name amid a thundering of applause. He stepped forth and cast a tender look in the direction of the fair maiden who had contrived to send him that tiny white bud that showed up so well on his black coat. He moved to the center of the platform and was lustily cheered, he walked with such superb grace and dignity.

He began his oration, capturing his audience with his first sentence and bearing them along on the powerful pinions of his masterly oratory; and when his peroration was over the audience drew its breath and cheered wildly for many, many minutes. He then proceeded to deliver the valedictory to the class. After he had been speaking for some time, his voice began to break with emotion. As he drew near to the most affecting portion he reached to his coat tail pocket to secure his silk handkerchief to brush away the gathering tears. As his hand left his pocket a smile was on well-nigh every face in the audience, but Belton did not see this, but with bowed head, proceeded with his pathetic utterances.

The audience of course was struggling between the pathos of his remarks and the humor of those dirty socks.

Belton's sweetheart began to cry from chagrin and his mother grew restless, anxious to tell him or let him know in some way. Belton's head continued bowed in sadness, as he spoke parting words to his beloved classmates, and lifted his supposed handkerchief to his eyes to wipe away the tears that were now coming freely. The socks had thus come close to Belton's nose and he stopped of a sudden and held them at arm's length to gaze at that terrible, terrible scent producer. When he saw what he held in his hand he flung them in front of him, they falling on some students, who hastily brushed them off.

The house, by this time, was in an uproar of laughter; and the astonished Belton gazed blankly at the socks lying before him. His mind was a mass of confusion. He hardly knew where he was or what he was doing. Self-possession, in a measure, returned to him, and he said: "Ladies and gentlemen, these socks are from Mississippi. I am from Virginia."

This reference to the Mississippian was greeted by an even louder outburst of laughter. Belton bowed and left the platform, murmuring that he would find and kill the rascal who had played that trick on him. The people saw the terrible frown on his face, and the president heard the revengeful words, and all feared that the incident was not closed.

Belton hurried out of the speakers' room and hastily ran to the city to purchase a pistol. Having secured it, he came walking back at a furious pace. By this time the exercises were over and friends were returning to town. They desired to approach Belton and compliment him, and urge him to look lightly on his humorous finale; but he looked so desperate that none dared to approach him.

The president was on the lookout for Belton and met him at the door of the boys' dormitory. He accosted Belton tenderly and placed his hand on his shoulder. Belton roughly pushed him aside and strode into the building and roamed through it, in search of his room-mate, whom he now felt assured did him the trick.

But his room-mate, foreseeing the consequences of detection, had made beforehand every preparation for leaving and was now gone. No one could quiet Belton during that whole day, and he spent the night meditating plans for wreaking vengeance.

The next morning the president came over early, and entering Belton's room, was more kindly received. He took Belton's hand in his and sat down near his side. He talked to Belton long and earnestly, showing him what an unholy passion revenge was. He showed that such a passion would mar any life that yielded to it.

Belton, he urged, was about to allow a pair of dirty socks to wreck his whole life. He drew a picture of the suffering Savior, crying out between darting pains the words of the sentence, the most sublime ever uttered: "Lord forgive them for they know not what they do." Belton was melted to tears of repentance for his unholy passion.

Before the president left Belton's side he felt sure that henceforth a cardinal principle of his life would be to allow God to avenge all his wrongs. It was a narrow escape for Belton, but he thanked God for the lesson, severe as it was, to the day of his death. The world will also see how much it owes to God for planting that lesson in Belton's heart.

Let us relate just one more incident that happened at the winding up of Belton's school life. As we have intimated, one young lady, a student of the school, was very near to Belton. Though he did not love her, his regard for her was very deep and his respect very great.

School closed on Thursday, and the students were allowed to remain in the buildings until the following Monday, when, ordinarily, they left. The young men were allowed to provide conveyances for the young ladies to get to the various depots. They esteemed that a very great privilege.

Belton, as you know, was a very poor lad and had but little money. After paying his expenses incident to his graduation, and purchasing a ticket home, he now had just one dollar and a quarter left. Out of this one dollar and a quarter he was to pay for a carriage ride of this young lady friend to the railway station. This, ordinarily, cost one dollar, and Belton calculated on having a margin of twenty-five cents. But you would have judged him the happy possessor of a large fortune, merely to look at him.

The carriage rolled up to the girls' dormitory and Belton's friend stood on the steps, with her trunks, three in number. When Belton saw that his friend had three trunks, his heart sank. In order to be sure against exorbitant charges the drivers were always made to announce their prices before the journey was commenced.

A crowd of girls was standing around to bid the young lady adieu. In an off-hand way Belton said: "Driver what is your fee?" He replied: "For you and the young lady and the trunks, two dollars, sir."

Belton almost froze in his tracks, but, by the most heroic struggling, showed no signs of discomfiture on his face. Endeavoring to affect an air of indifference, he said: "What is the price for the young lady and the trunks?"

"One dollar and fifty cents."

Belton's eyes were apparently fixed on some spot in the immensity of space. The driver, thinking that he was meditating getting another hackman to do the work, added: "You can call any hackman you choose and you won't find one who will do it for a cent less."

Belton's last prop went with this statement. He turned to his friend smilingly and told her to enter, with apparently as much indifference as a millionaire. He got in and sat by her side; but knew not how on earth he was to get out of his predicament.

The young lady chatted gayly and wondered at Belton's dullness. Belton, poor fellow, was having a tough wrestle with poverty and was trying to coin something out of nothing. Now and then, at some humorous remark, he would smile a faint, sickly smile. Thus it went on until they arrived at the station. Belton by this time decided upon a plan of campaign.

They alighted from the carriage and Belton escorted his friend into the coach. He then came back to speak to the driver. He got around the corner of the station house, out of sight of the train and beckoned for the driver to come to him. The driver came and Belton said: "Friend, here is one dollar and a quarter. It is all I have. Trust me for the balance until tomorrow."

"Oh! no," replied the driver. "I must have my money to-day. I have to report to-night and my money must go in. Just fork over the balance, please."

"Well," said Belton rather independently—for he felt that he now had the upper hand,—"I have given you all the money that I have. And you have got to trust me for the balance. You can't take us back," and Belton started to walk away.

The driver said: "May be that girl has some money. I'll see her."

Terror immediately seized Belton, and he clutched at the man eagerly, saying: "Ah, no, now, don't resort to any such foolishness. Can't you trust a fellow?" Belton was now talking very persuasively.

The driver replied: "I don't do business that way. If I had known that you did not have the money I would not have brought you. I am going to the young lady."

Belton was now thoroughly frightened and very angry; and he planted himself squarely in front of the driver and said: "You shall do no such thing!"

The driver heard the train blow and endeavored to pass. Belton grasped him by the collar and putting a leg quickly behind him, tripped him to the ground, falling on top of him. The driver struggled, but Belton succeeded in getting astride of him and holding him down. The train shortly pulled out, and Belton jumped up and ran to wave a good-bye to his girl friend.

Later in the day, the driver had him arrested and the police justice fined him ten dollars. A crowd of white men who heard Belton's story, admired his respect for the girl, and paid the fine for him and made up a purse.

At Stowe University, Belton had learned to respect women. It was in these schools that the work of slavery in robbing the colored women of respect, was undone. Woman now occupied the same position in Belton's eye as she did in the eye of the Anglo-Saxon.

There is hope for that race or nation that respects its women. It was for the smile of a woman that the armored knight of old rode forth to deeds of daring. It is for the smile of women that the soldier of to-day endures the hardships of the camp and braves the dangers of the field of battle.

The heart of man will joyfully consent to be torn to pieces if the lovely hand of woman will only agree to bind the parts together again and heal the painful wounds.

The Negro race had left the last relic of barbarism behind, and this young negro, fighting to keep that cab driver from approaching the girl for a fee, was but a forerunner of the negro, who, at the voice of a woman, will fight for freedom until he dies, fully satisfied if the hand that he worships will only drop a flower on his grave.

Belton's education was now complete, as far as the school-room goes.

What will he do with it?

CHAPTER VIII

MANY MYSTERIES CLEARED UP

On the day prior to the one on which Bernard first entered the public school of Winchester, Fairfax Belgrave had just arrived in the town.

A costly residence, beautifully located and furnished in the most luxurious manner, was on the eve of being sold. Mrs. Belgrave purchased this house and installed herself as mistress thereof. Here she lived in isolation with her boy, receiving no callers and paying no visits. Being a devoted Catholic, she attended all the services of her church and reared Bernard in that faith.

For a time white and colored people speculated much as to who Mrs. Belgrave was, and as to what was the source of her revenue; for she was evidently a woman of wealth. She employed many servants and these were plied with thousands of questions by people of both races. But the life of Mrs. Belgrave was so circumspect, so far removed from anything suspicious, and her bearing was so evidently that of a woman of pure character and high ideals that speculation died out after a year or two, and the people gave up the finding out of her history as a thing impossible of achievement. With seemingly unlimited money at her command, all of Bernard's needs were supplied and his lightest wishes gratified. Mrs. Belgrave was a woman with very superior education. The range of her reading was truly remarkable. She possessed the finest library ever seen in the northern section of Virginia, and all the best of the latest books were constantly arriving at her home. Magazines and newspapers arrived by every mail. Thus she was thoroughly abreast with the times.

As Bernard grew up, he learned to value associating with his mother above every other pleasure. She superintended his literary training and cultivated in him a yearning for literature of the highest and purest type. Politics, science, art, religion, sociology, and, in fact, the whole realm of human knowledge was invaded and explored. Such home training was an invaluable supplement to what Bernard received in school. When, therefore, he entered Harvard, he at once moved to the front rank in every particular. Many white young men of wealth and high social standing, attracted by his brilliancy, drew near him and became his fast friends. In his graduating year, he was so popular as to be elected president of his class, and so scholarly as to be made valedictorian.

These achievements on his part were so remarkable that the Associated Press telegraphed the news over the country, and many were the laudatory notices that he received. The night of his graduation, when he had finished delivering his oration that swept all before it as does the whirlwind and the hurricane, as he stepped out of the door to take his carriage for home, a tall man with a broad face and long flowing beard stepped up behind him and tapped him on the shoulder.

Bernard turned and the man handed him a note. Tearing the envelope open he saw in his mother's well known handwriting the following:

"DEAR BERNIE:

"Follow this man and trust him as you would your loving mother.

"FAIRFAX BELGRAVE."

Bernard dismissed his carriage, ordered to take him to his lodging, and spoke to the man who had accosted him, saying that he was at his service. They walked a distance and soon were at the railroad station. They boarded the train and in due time arrived in Washington, D.C., Bernard asking no questions, knowing that a woman as habitually careful as his mother did not send that message without due care and grave purpose.

In Washington they took a carriage and were driven to one of the most fashionable portions of the city, and stopped before a mansion of splendid appearance. Bernard's escort led the way into the house, having a key to which all of the doors responded. Bernard was left in the parlor and told to remain until some one called for him. The tall man with long flowing beard went to his room and removed his disguise.

In a few minutes a negro servant, sent by this man, appeared and led Bernard to a room in the rear of the house on the second floor. It was a large room having two windows, one facing the east and the other the north.

As he stepped into the room he saw sitting directly facing him a white man, tall and of a commanding appearance. His hair, and for that matter his whole noble looking head and handsome face bore a striking resemblance to Bernard's own. The latter perceived the likeness and halted in astonishment. The man arose and handed Bernard a note. Bernard opened it and found it exactly resembling the one handed him just prior to his journey to Washington.

The man eyed Bernard from head to foot with a look that betrayed the keenest interest. Opening one of the drawers of his desk he drew forth a paper. It was a marriage certificate, certifying to a marriage between Fairfax Belgrave and ————.

"I am your mother's lawful husband, and you are my legitimate child."

Bernard knew not what to say, think, or feel. His mother had so carefully avoided any mention of her family affairs that he regarded them as among things sacred, and he never allowed even his thoughts to wander in that direction.

"I am Senator ———— from the state of ————, chairman of ———— committee."

The information contained in that sentence made Bernard rise from his seat with a bound. The man's name was a household word throughout the nation, and his reputation was international.

"Be seated, Bernard, I have much to say to you. I have a long story to tell. I have been married twice. My first wife's brother was Governor of ———— and lived and died a bachelor. He was, however, the father of a child, whose mother was a servant connected with his father's household. The child was given to my wife to rear, and she accepted the charge. The child bloomed into a perfect beauty, possessed a charming voice, could perform with extraordinary skill on the piano, and seemed to have inherited the mind of her father, whose praises have been sung in all the land.

"When this child was seventeen years of age my wife died. This girl remained in our house. I was yet a young man. Now that my wife was gone, attending to this girl fell entirely into my hands. I undertook her education. As her mind unfolded, so many beauteous qualities appeared that she excited my warm admiration.

"By chance, I discovered that the girl loved me; not as a father, but as she would a lover. She does not know to this day that I made the discovery when I did. As for myself, I had for some time been madly in love with her. When I discovered that my affections were returned, I made proposals, at that time regarded as honorable enough by the majority of white men of the South.

"It seemed as though my proposition did not take her by surprise. She gently, but most firmly rejected my proposal. She told me that the proposal was of a nature to occasion deep and lasting repugnance, but that in my case she blamed circumstances and conditions more than she did me. The quiet, loving manner in which she resented insult and left no tinge of doubt as to her virtue, if possible, intensified my love. A few days later she came to me and said: 'Let us go to Canada and get married secretly. I will return South with you. No one shall ever know what we have done, and for the sake of your political and social future I will let the people apply whatever name they wish to our relationship.'

"I gladly embraced the proposal, knowing that she would keep faith even unto death; although I realized how keenly her pure soul felt at being regarded as living with me dishonorably. Yet, love and interest bade her bow her head and receive the public mark of shame.

"Heroic soul! That is the marriage certificate which I showed you. You were born. When you were four years old your mother told me that she must leave, as she could not bear to see her child grow up esteeming her an adulteress.

"The war broke out, and I entered the army, and your mother took you to Europe, where she lived until the war was over, when she returned to Winchester, Virginia. Her father was a man of wealth, and you own two millions of dollars through your mother. At my death you shall have eight millions more.

"So much for the past. Let me tell you of my plans and hopes for your future. This infernal race prejudice has been the curse of my life. Think of my pure-hearted, noble-minded wife, branded as a harlot, and you, my own son, stigmatized as a bastard, because it would be suicide for me to let the world know that you both are mine, though you both are the direct descendants of a governor, and a long line of heroes whose names are ornaments to our nation's history.

"I want you to break down this prejudice. It is the wish of your mother and your father. You must move in the front, but all that money and quiet influence can do shall be done by me for your advancement. I paid Mr. Tiberius Gracchus Leonard two thousand dollars a year to teach you at Winchester. His is a master mind. One rash deed robbed the world of seeing a colossal intellect in high station. I shall tell you his history presently.

"I desire you to go to Norfolk County, Virginia, and hang up your sign as an attorney at law. I wish you to run for congress from that district. Leonard is down there. As you will find out, he will be of inestimable service to you.

"Now let me give you his history. Leonard was the most brilliant student that ever entered ———— University in the state of ————. Just prior to the time when he would have finished his education at school, the war broke out and he enlisted in the Confederate Army, and was made a colonel of a regiment. I was also a colonel, and when our ranks became depleted the two regiments were thrown into one. Though he was the ranking officer, our commander, as gallant and intrepid an officer as ever trod a battle field, was put in command. This deeply humilitated Leonard and he swore to be avenged.

"One evening, when night had just lowered her black wings over the earth, we were engaging the enemy. Our commander was in advance of his men. Suddenly the commander fell, wounded. At first it was thought that the enemy had shot him, but investigation showed that the ball had entered his back. It was presumed, then, that some of his own men had mistook him for an enemy and had shot him through mistake. Leonard had performed the nefarious deed knowingly. By some skillful detective work, I secured incontestible evidence of his guilt. I went to him with my proof and informed him of my intentions to lay it before a superior officer. His answer was: 'If you do, I will let the whole world know about your nigger wife.' I fell back as if stunned. Terror seized me. If he knew of my marriage might not others know it? Might not it be already generally known? These were the thoughts that coursed through my brain. However, with an effort I suppressed my alarm. Seeing that each possessed a secret that meant death and disgrace to the other (for I shall certainly kill myself if I am ever exposed) I entered into an agreement with him.

"On the condition that he would prepare a statement confessing his guilt and detailing the circumstances of the crime and put this paper in my hand, I would show him my marriage certificate; and after that, each was to regard the other's secret as inviolate.

"We thus held each other securely tied. His conscience, however, disturbed him beyond measure; and every evening, just after dusk, he fancied that he saw the form of his departed commander. It made him cowardly in battle and he at last deserted.

"He informed me as to how my secret came into his possession. Soon after he committed his crime he felt sure that I was in possession of his secret, and he thought to steal into my tent and murder me. He stole in there one night to perpetrate the crime. I was talking in my sleep. In my slumber I told the story of my secret marriage in such circumstantial detail that it impressed him as being true. Feeling that he could hold me with that, he spared my life, determined to wound me deeper than death if I struck at him.

"You see that he is a cowardly villain; but we sometimes have to use such.

"Now, my son, go forth; labor hard and climb high. Scale the high wall of prejudice. Make it possible, dear boy, for me to own you ere I pass out of life. Let your mother have the veil of slander torn from her pure form ere she closes her eyes on earth forever."

Bernard, handsome, brilliant, eloquent, the grandson of a governor, the son of a senator, a man of wealth, to whom defeat was a word unknown, steps out to battle for the freedom of his race;

urged to put his whole soul into the fight because of his own burning desire for glory, and because out of the gloom of night he heard his grief stricken parents bidding him to climb where the cruel world would be compelled to give its sanction to the union that produced such a man as he.

Bernard's training was over. He now had a tremendous incentive. Into life he plunges.

CHAPTER IX

LOVE AND POLITICS

Acting on his father's advice Bernard arrived in Norfolk in the course of a few days. He realized that he was now a politician and decided to make a diligent study of the art of pleasing the populace and to sacrifice everything to the goddess of fame. Knowing that whom the people loved they honored, he decided to win their love at all hazards. He decided to become the obedient servant of the people that he might thus make all the people his servants.

He took up his abode at Hotel Douglass, a colored hotel at which the colored leaders would often congregate. Bernard mingled with these men freely and soon had the name among them of being a jovial good fellow.

While at Harvard, Bernard had studied law simultaneously with his other studies and graduated from both the law and classical departments the same year.

Near the city court house, in a row of somewhat dilapidated old buildings, he rented a law office. The rowdy and criminal element infested this neighborhood. Whenever any of these got into difficulties, Bernard was always ready to defend them. If they were destitute of funds he would serve them free of charge and would often pay their fines for them. He was ever ready to go on bonds of any who got into trouble. He gave money freely to those who begged of him. In this manner he became the very ideal of the vicious element, though not accounted by them as one of their number.

Bernard was also equally successful in winning favor with the better element of citizens. Though a good Catholic at heart, he divided his time among all denominations, thus solving the most difficult problem for a Negro leader to solve; for the religious feeling was so intense that it was carried into almost every branch of human activity.

Having won the criminal and religious circles, he thought to go forth and conquer the social world and secure its support. He decided to enter society and pay marked attention to that young lady that would most increase his popularity. We shall soon see how this would-be conqueror stood the very first fire.

His life had been one of such isolation that he had not at all moved in social circles before this, and no young woman had ever made more than a passing impression on him.

There was in Norfolk a reading circle composed of the brightest, most talented young men and women of the city. Upon taking a short vacation, this circle always gave a reception which was attended by persons of the highest culture in the city. Bernard received an invitation to this reception, and, in company with a fellow lawyer attended. The reception was held at the residence of a Miss Evangeline Leslie, a member of the circle.

The house was full of guests when Bernard and his friend arrived. They rang the door bell and a young lady came to the door to receive them.

She was a small, beautifully formed girl with a luxuriant growth of coal black hair that was arranged in such a way as to impart a queenly look to her shapely head. Her skin was dark brown, tender and smooth in appearance. A pair of laughing hazel eyes, a nose of the prettiest possible size and shape, and a chin that tapered with the most exquisite beauty made her face the Mecca of all eyes.

Bernard was so struck with the girl's beauty that he did not greet her when she opened the door. He stared at her with a blank look. They were invited in.

Bernard pulled off his hat and walked in, not saying a word but eyeing that pretty girl all the while. Even when his back was turned toward her, as he walked, his head was turned over his shoulders and his eye surveyed all the graceful curves of her perfect form and scanned those features that could but charm those who admire nature's work.

When he had taken a seat in the corner of a room by the side of his friend he said: "Pray, who is that girl that met you at the door? I really did not know that a dark woman could look so beautiful."

"You are not the only one that thinks that she is surpassingly beautiful," said his friend. "Her picture is the only Negro's picture that is allowed to hang in the show glasses of the white photographers down town. White and colored pay homage to her beauty."

"Well," said Bernard, "that man who denies that girl's beauty should be sent to the asylum for the cure of a perverted and abnormal taste."

"I see you are rather enthusiastic. Is it wise to admire mortgaged property?" remarked his friend.

"What's that?" asked Bernard, quickly. "Is any body in my way?"

"In your way?" laughed his friend. "Pray what do you mean? I don't understand you."

"Come," said Bernard, "I am on pins. Is she married or about to be?"

"Well, not exactly that, but she has told me that she cares a good bit for me."

Bernard saw that his friend was in a mood to tease him and he arose and left his side.

His friend chuckled gleefully to himself and said: "The would-be catcher is caught. I thought Viola Martin would duck him if anybody could. Tell me about these smile-proof bachelors. When once they are struck, they fall all to pieces at once."

Bernard sought his landlady, who was present as a guest, and through her secured an introduction to Miss Viola Martin. He found her even more beautiful, if possible, in mind than in form and he sat conversing with her all the evening as if enchanted.

The people present were not at all surprised; for as soon as Bernard's brilliancy and worth were known in the town and people began to love him, it was generally hoped and believed that Miss Martin would take him captive at first sight.

Miss Viola Martin was a universal favorite. She was highly educated and an elocutionist of no mean ability. She sang sweetly and was the most accomplished pianist in town. She was bubbling over with good humor and her wit and funny stories were the very life of any circle where she happened to be. She was most remarkably well-informed on all leading questions of the day, and men of brain always enjoyed a chat with her. And the children and older people fairly worshipped her; for she paid especial attention to these. In all religious movements among the women she was the leading spirit.

With all these points in her favor she was unassuming and bowed her head so low that the darts of jealousy, so universally hurled at the brilliant and popular, never came her way. No one in Norfolk was considered worthy of her heart and hand and the community was tenderly solicitous as to who should wed her.

Bernard had made such rapid strides in their affections and esteem that they had already assigned him to their pet, Viola, or Vie as she was popularly called.

When the time for the departure of the guests arrived, Bernard with great regret bade Miss Martin adieu.

She ran upstairs to get her cloak, and a half dozen girls went tripping up stairs behind her; when once in the room set apart for the ladies' cloaks they began to gleefully pound Viola with pillows and smother her with kisses.

"You have made a catch, Vie. Hold him," said one.

"He'll hold himself," said another. To all of which Viola answered with a sigh.

A mulatto girl stepped up to Viola and with a merry twinkle in her eye said: "Theory is theory and practice is practice, eh, Vie? Well, we would hardly blame you in this case."

Viola earnestly replied: "I shall ask for no mercy. Theory and practice are one with me in this case."

"Bah, bah, girl, two weeks will change that tune. And I, for one, won't blame you," replied the mulatto still in a whisper.

The girls seeing that Viola did not care to be teased about Bernard soon ceased, and she came down stairs to be escorted home by the young man who had accompanied her there.

This young man was, thus early, jealous of Bernard and angry at Viola for receiving his attentions, and as a consequence he was silent all the way home.

This gave Viola time to think of that handsome, talented lawyer whom she had just met. She had to confess to herself that he had aroused considerable interest in her bosom and she looked forward to a promised visit with pleasure. But every now and then a sigh would escape her, such as she made when the girls were teasing her.

Her escort bade her good-night at her father's gate in a most sullen manner, but Viola was so lost in thought that she did not notice it. She entered the house feeling lively and cheerful, but when she entered her room she burst into crying. She would laugh a while and cry a while as though she had a foretaste of coming bliss mixed with bitterness.

Bernard at once took the place left vacant by the dropping away of the jealous young man and became Viola's faithful attendant, accompanying her wherever he could. The more he met Viola, the more beautiful she appeared to him and the more admirable he found her mind.

Bernard almost forgot his political aspirations, and began to ponder that passage of scripture that said man should not be alone. But he did not make such progress with Viola as was satisfactory to him. Sometimes she would appear delighted to see him and was all life and gayety. Again she was scarcely more than polite and seemed perfectly indifferent to him.

After a long while Bernard decided that Viola, who seemed to be very ambitious, treated him thus because he had not done anything worthy of special note. He somewhat slacked up in his attentions and began to devote himself to acquiring wide spread popularity with a view to entering Congress and reaching Viola in this way.

The more he drew off from Viola the more friendly she would seem to him, and he began to feel that seeming indifference was perhaps the way to win her. Thus the matter moved along for a couple of years.

In the meantime, Mr. Tiberius Gracchus Leonard, Bernard's old teacher, was busy in Norfolk looking after Bernard's political interests, acting under instructions from Bernard's father, Senator —————.

About this stage of Bernard's courtship Mr. Leonard called on him and told him that the time was ripe for Bernard to announce himself for Congress. Bernard threw his whole soul into the project. He had another great incentive to cause him to wish to succeed, Viola Martin's hand and heart.

In order to understand what followed we must now give a bit of Virginia political history.

In the year ————— there was a split in the democratic party of Virginia on the question of paying Virginia's debt to England. The bolting section of the party joined hands with the republicans and whipped the regular democrats at the polls. This coalition thus formed was eventually made the Republican party of Virginia.

The democrats, however, rallied and swept this coalition from power and determined to forever hold the state government if they had to resort to fraud. They resorted to ballot box stuffing and various other means to maintain control. At last, they passed a law creating a state electoral commission.

This commission was composed of three democrats. These three democrats were given the power to appoint three persons in each county as an Electoral Board. These county electoral boards would appoint judges for each precinct or voting place in the county. They would also appoint a special constable at each voting booth to assist the illiterate voters.

With rare exceptions, the officials were democrats, and with the entire state's election machinery in their hands the democrats could manage elections according to their "own sweet will." It goes without saying that the democrats always carried any and every precinct that they decided, and elections were mere farces.

Such was the condition of affairs when Bernard came forward as a candidate from the Second Congressional District. The district was overwhelmingly republican, but the democrats always secured the office.

It was regarded as downright foolhardy to attempt to get elected to Congress from the District as a republican; so the nomination was merely passed around as an honor, empty enough.

It was such a feeling that inspired the republicans to nominate Bernard; but Bernard entered the canvass in dead earnest and conducted a brilliant campaign.

The masses of colored people rallied around his flag. Ministers of colored churches came to his support. Seeing that the colored people were so determined to elect Bernard, the white republicans, leaders and followers, fell into line. Viola Martin organized patriotic clubs among the women and aroused whatever voters seemed lethargic.

The day of election came and Bernard was elected by a majority of 11,823 votes; but the electoral boards gave the certificate of election to his opponent, alleging his opponent's majority to be 4,162.

Bernard decided to contest the election in Congress, and here is where Leonard's fine work was shown. He had, for sometime, made it appear in Norfolk that he was a democrat of the most radical school. The leading democrats made his acquaintance and Leonard very often composed speeches for them. He thus became a favorite with certain prominent democrats and they let him into the secret workings of the electoral machinery. Thus informed, Leonard went to headquarters of the Democratic party at Richmond with a view to bribing the clerks to give him inside facts. He found the following to be the character of the work done at headquarters.

A poll of all the voters in the state was made. The number of white and the number of colored voters in each voting precinct was secured. The number of illiterate voters of both races was ascertained. With these facts in their possession, they had conducted all the campaign necessary for them to carry on an election. Of course speakers were sent out as a sham, but they were not needed for anything more than appearances.

Having the figures indicated above before them, they proceeded to assign to each district, each county, each city, each precinct just such majorities as they desired, taking pains to make the figures appear reasonable and differ somewhat from figures of previous years. Whenever it would do no harm, a precinct was granted to the republicans for the sake of appearances.

Ballot boxes of varied patterns were secured and filled with ballots marked just as they desired. Some ballots were for republicans, some for democrats, and some marked wrong so as to indicate the votes of illiterates. The majorities, of course, were invariably such as suited the democrats. The ballots were all carefully counted and arranged; and tabulated statements of the votes cast put in. A sheet for the returns was put in, only awaiting the signatures of the officials at the various precincts in order to be complete. These boxes were carried by trusted messengers to their destinations.

On election day, not these boxes, but boxes similar to them were used to receive the ballots. On the night of the election, the ballot boxes that actually received the votes were burned with all their contents and the boxes and ballots from Richmond were substituted. The judges of election took out the return sheet, already prepared, signed it and returned it to Richmond forthwith. Thus it could always be known thirty days ahead just what the exact vote in detail was to be throughout the entire state. In fact a tabulated statement was prepared and printed long before election day.

Leonard paid a clerk at headquarters five thousand dollars for one of these tabulated statements. With this he hurried on to Washington and secretly placed it before the Republican Congressional Campaign Committee, with the understanding that it was to be used after election day as a basis for possible contest. Fifteen of the most distinguished clergymen in the nation were summoned to Washington and made affidavits, stating that they had seen this tabulated statement twenty days before the election took place.

When Virginia's returns came in they were found to correspond in every detail to this tabulated report.

As nothing but a prophet, direct from God, could have foreseen the results exactly as they did occur, this tabulated statement was proof positive of fraud on a gigantic scale.

With this and a mass of other indisputable evidence at his back, secured by the shrewd Leonard, Bernard entered the contest for his seat. The House of Representatives was democratic by a small majority. The contest was a long and bitter one. The republicans were solidly for Bernard. The struggle was eagerly watched from day to day. It was commonly believed that the democrats would vote against Bernard, despite the clear case in his favor.

The day to vote on the contest at last arrived and the news was flashed over the country that Bernard had triumphed. A handful of democrats had deserted their party and voted with the republicans. Bernard's father had redeemed his promise of secret support. Bernard's triumph in a democratic house caused the nation to rub its eyes and look again in wonder.

The colored people hailed Bernard as the coming Moses. "Belgrave, Belgrave, Belgrave," was on every Negro tongue. Poems were addressed to him. Babies were named after him. Honorary titles were showered upon him. He was in much demand at fairs and gatherings of notable people. He accepted every invitation of consequence, whenever possible, and traveled far and wide winning friends by his bewitching eloquence and his pleasing personality.

The democrats, after that defeat, always passed the second district by and Bernard held his seat in Congress from year to year unmolested. He made application and was admitted to plead law before the Supreme Court of the United States. And when we shall see him again it will be there, pleading in one of the most remarkable cases known to jurisprudence.

CHAPTER X

CUPID AGAIN AT WORK

Belton, after graduating from Stowe University, returned with his mother to their humble home at Winchester. He had been away at school for four years and now desired to see his home again before going forth into the world.

He remained at Winchester several days visiting all the spots where he had toiled or played, mourned or sung, wept or laughed as a child. He entered the old school house and gazed with eyes of love on its twisting walls, decaying floor and benches sadly in need of repair. A somewhat mournful smile played upon his lips as he thought of the revengeful act that he had perpetrated upon his first teacher, Mr. Leonard, and this smile died away into a more sober expression as he remembered how his act of revenge had, like chickens, come home to roost, when those dirty socks had made him an object of laughter at Stowe University on commencement day.

Revenge was dead in his bosom. And it was well for the world that this young negro had been trained in a school where there was a friendly lance to open his veins and let out this most virulent of poisons.

Belton lingered about home, thinking of the great problem of human life. He would walk out of town near sunset and, taking his seat on some grassy knoll would gaze on the Blue Ridge mountains. The light would fade out of the sky and the gloom of evening gather, but the mountains would maintain their same bold appearance. Whenever he cast his eyes in their direction, there they stood firm and immovable.

His pure and lofty soul had an affinity for all things grand and he was always happy, even from childhood, when he could sit undisturbed and gaze at the mountains, huge and lofty, rising in such unconquerable grandeur, upward toward the sky. Belton chose the mountain as the emblem of his life and he besought God to make him such in the moral world.

At length he tore himself loose from the scenes of his childhood, and embracing his fond mother, left Winchester to begin life in the city of Richmond, the capital of the old Confederacy. Through the influence of Mr. King, his benefactor, he secured a position as a teacher in one of the colored schools of that city.

The principal of the school to which Belton was assigned was white, but all the rest of the teachers were young colored women. On the morning of his arrival at the school building Belton was taken in charge by the principal, and by him was carried around to be introduced to the various teachers. Before he reaches a certain room, let us give you a slight introduction to the occupant thereof.

Antoinette Nermal was famed throughout the city for her beauty, intelligence and virtue. Her color was what is termed a light brown skin. We assure you that it was charming enough. She was of medium height, and for grace and symmetry her form was fit for a sculptor's model. Her pretty face bore the stamp of intellectuality, but the intellectuality of a beautiful woman, who was still every inch a woman despite her intellectuality. Her thin well-formed lips seemed arranged by nature in such a manner as to be incomplete without a kiss, and that lovely face seemed to reinforce the invitation. Her eyes were black, and when you gazed in them the tenderness therein seemed to be about to draw you out of yourself. They concealed and yet revealed a heart capable of passionate love.

Those who could read her and wished her well were much concerned that she should love wisely; for it could be seen that she was to love with her whole heart, and to wreck her love was to wreck her life. She had passed through all her life thus far without seriously noticing any young man, thus giving some the impression that she was incapable of love, being so intellectual. Others who read her better knew that she despised the butterfly, flitting from flower to flower, and was preserving her heart to give it whole into the keeping of some worthy man.

She neither sang nor played, but her soul was intensely musical and she had the most refined and cultivated taste in the musical circles in which she moved. She was amiable in disposition, but her amiability was not of the kind to lead her in quest of you; but if you came across her, she would treat you so pleasantly that you would desire to pass that way again.

Belton and the principal are now on the way to her room. As they entered the door her back was to them, as she was gazing out of the window. Belton's eyes surveyed her graceful form and he was so impressed with its loveliness that he was sorry when she began to turn around. But when she was turned full around Belton forgot all about her form, and his eyes did not know which to contemplate longest, that rich complexion, those charming eyes, or those seductive lips. On the other hand, Miss Nermal was struck with Belton's personal appearance and as she contemplated the noble, dignified yet genial appearance which he presented, her lips came slightly apart, rendering her all the more beautiful.

The principal said: "Miss Nermal, allow me to present to you our newly arrived associate in the work, Mr. Belton Piedmont."

Miss Nermal smiled to Belton and said: "Mr. Piedmont, we are glad to have a man of your acknowledged talents in our midst and we anticipate much of you."

Belton felt much flattered, surprised, overjoyed. He wished that he could find the person who had been so very kind as to give that marvelously beautiful girl such a good opinion of himself. But when he opened his mouth to reply he was afraid of saying something that would shatter this good opinion; so he bowed politely and merely said, "Thank you."

"I trust that you will find our association agreeable," said Miss Nermal, smiling and walking toward him.

This remark turned Belton's mind to thoughts that stimulated him to a brisk reply. "Oh assuredly, Miss Nermal. I am already more than satisfied that I shall expect much joy and pleasure from my association with you—I—I—I mean the teachers."

Belton felt that he had made a bad break and looked around a little uneasily at the principal, violently condemning in his heart that rule which led principals to escort young men around; especially when there was a likelihood of meeting with such a lovely girl. If you had consulted Belton's wishes at that moment, school would have been adjourned immediately, the principal excused, and himself allowed to look at and talk to Miss Nermal as much as he desired.

However, this was not to be. The principal moved to the door to continue his tour. Belton reluctantly followed. He didn't see the need of getting acquainted with all the teachers in one day. He thought that there were too many teachers in that building, anyhow. These were Belton's rebellious thoughts as he left Miss Nermal's room.

Nevertheless, he finished his journey around to the various rooms and afterwards assumed charge of his own room. Some might ascribe his awkwardness in his room that day to the fact that the work was new to him. But we prefer to think that certain new and pleasing sensations in his bosom were responsible.

When the young lady teachers got together at noon that day, the question was passed around as to what was thought of Mr. Piedmont. Those teachers whom Belton met before he entered Miss Nermal's room thought him "very nice." Those whom he met after he left her room thought him rather dull. Miss Nermal herself pronounced him "just grand."

All of the girls looked at Miss Nermal rather inquiringly when she said this, for she was understood to usually pass young men by unnoticed. Each of the other girls, previous to seeing Belton, had secretly determined to capture the rising young orator in case his personal appearance kept pace with his acknowledged talents. In debating the matter they had calculated their chances of success and had thought of all possible rivals. Miss Nermal was habitually so indifferent to young men that they had not considered her as a possibility. They were quite surprised, to say the least, to hear her speak more enthusiastically of Belton than any of the rest had done. If Miss Nermal was to be their rival they were ready to abandon the field at once, for the charms of her face, form, and mind were irresistible when in repose; and what would they be if she became interested in winning the heart of a young man?

When school was dismissed that afternoon Belton saw a group of teachers walking homeward and Miss Nermal was in the group. Belton joined them and somehow contrived to get by Miss Nermal's side. How much she aided him by unobserved shifting of positions is not known.

All of the rest of the group lived nearer the school than did Miss Nermal and so, when they had all dropped off at respective gates, Miss Nermal yet had some distance to go. When Belton saw this, he was a happy fellow. He felt that the parents of the teachers had shown such excellent judgment in choosing places to reside. He would not have them change for the world. He figured that he would have five evenings of undisturbed bliss in each week walking home with Miss Nermal after the other teachers had left.

Belton contrived to walk home with the same group each evening. The teachers soon noticed that Miss Nermal and Belton invariably walked together, and they managed by means of various excuses to break up the group; and Belton had the unalloyed pleasure of escorting Miss Nermal from the school-house door to her own front yard. Belton secured the privilege of calling to see Miss Nermal at her residence and he confined his social visits to her house solely.

They did not talk of love to one another, but any one who saw the couple together could tell at a glance what was in each heart. Belton, however, did not have the courage to approach the subject. His passion was so intense and absorbing and filled him with so much delight that he feared to talk on the subject so dear to his heart, for fear of a repulse and the shattering of all the beautiful castles which his glowing imagination, with love as the supervising architect, had constructed. Thus matters moved along for some time; Miss Nermal thoroughly in love with Belton, but Belton prizing that love too highly to deem it possible for him to be the happy possessor thereof.

Belton was anxious for some indirect test. He would often contrive little devices to test Miss Nermal's feelings toward him and in each case the result was all that he could wish, yet he doubted. Miss Nermal thoroughly understood Belton and was anxious for him to find some way out of his dilemma. Of course it was out of the question for her to volunteer to tell him that she loved him—loved him madly, passionately; loved him in every fibre of her soul.

At last the opportunity that Belton was hoping for came. Miss Nermal and Belton were invited out to a social gathering of young people one night. He was Miss Nermal's escort.

At this gathering the young men and women played games such

as pinning on the donkey's tail, going to Jerusalem, menagerie, and various other parlor games. In former days, these social gatherings played some games that called for kissing by the young ladies and gentlemen, but Miss Nermal had opposed such games so vigorously that they had long since been dismissed from the best circles.

Belton had posted two or three young men to suggest a play involving kissing, that play being called, "In the well." The suggestion was made and just for the fun of having an old time game played, they accepted the suggestion. The game was played as follows.

Young men and young women would move their chairs as close back to the walls as possible. This would leave the center of the room clear. A young man would take his place in the middle of the floor and say, "I am in the well." A questioner would then ask, "How many feet?" The party in the well would then say, for instance, "Three feet." The questioner would then ask, "Whom will you have to take you out?"

Whosoever was named by the party in the well was required by the rules of the game to go to him and kiss him the number of times equivalent to the number of feet he was in the well.

The party thus called would then be in the well. The young men would kiss the ladies out and vice versa.

Miss Nermal's views on kissing games were well known and the young men all passed her by. Finally, a young lady called Belton to the well to kiss her out. Belton now felt that his chance had come. He was so excited that when he went to the well he forgot to kiss her. Belton was not conscious of the omission but it pleased Antoinette immensely.

Belton said, "I am in the well." The questioner asked, "How many feet?" Belton replied, "*only* one." "Whom will you have to take you out?" queried the questioner. Belton was in a dazed condition. He was astounded at his own temerity in having deliberately planned to call Miss Nermal to kiss him before that crowd or for that matter to kiss him at all. However he decided to make a bold dash. He averted his head and said, "Miss Antoinette Nermal."

All eyes were directed to Miss Nermal to see her refuse. But she cast a look of defiance around the room and calmly walked to where Belton stood. Their eyes met. They understood each other. Belton pressed those sweet lips that had been taunting him all those many days and sat down, the happiest of mortals.

Miss Nermal was now left in the well to call for some one to take her out. For the first time, it dawned upon Belton that in working to secure a kiss for himself, he was about to secure one for some one else also. He glared around the room furiously and wondered who would be base enough to dare to go and kiss that angel.

Miss Nermal was proceeding with her part of the game and Belton began to feel that she did not mind it even if she did have to kiss some one else. After all, he thought, his test would not hold good as she was, he felt sure, about to kiss another.

While Belton was in agony over such thoughts Miss Nermal came to the point where she had to name her deliverer. She said, "The person who put me in here will have to take me out." Belton bounded from his seat and, if the fervor of a kiss could keep the young lady in the well from drowning, Miss Nermal was certainly henceforth in no more danger.

Miss Nermal's act broke up that game.

On the way home that night, neither Antoinette nor Belton spoke a word. Their hearts were too full for utterance. When they reached Miss Nermal's gate, she opened it and entering stood on the other side, facing Belton.

Belton looked down into her beautiful face and she looked up at Belton. He felt her eyes pulling at the cords of his heart. He stooped down and in silence pressed a lingering kiss on Miss Nermal's lips. She did not move.

Belton said, "I am in the well." Miss Nermal whispered, "I am too." Belton said, "I shall always be in the well." Miss Nermal said, "So shall I." Belton hastily plucked open the gate and clasped Antoinette to his bosom. He led her to a double seat in the middle of the lawn, and there with the pure-eyed stars gazing down upon them they poured out their love to each other.

Two hours later Belton left her and at that late hour roused every intimate friend that he had in the city to tell them of his good fortune.

Miss Nermal was no less reserved in her joy. She told the good news everywhere to all her associates. Love had transformed this modest, reserved young woman into a being that would not have hesitated to declare her love upon a house-top.

CHAPTER XI

No Befitting Name

Happy Belton now began to give serious thought to the question of getting married. He desired to lead Antoinette to the altar as soon as possible and then he would be sure of possessing the richest treasure known to earth. And when he would speak of an early marriage she would look happy and say nothing in discouragement of the idea. She was Belton's, and she did not care how soon he claimed her as his own.

His poverty was his only barrier. His salary was small, being only fifty dollars a month. He had not held his position long enough to save up very much money. He decided to start up an enterprise that would enable him to make money a great deal faster.

The colored people of Richmond at that time had no newspaper or printing office. Belton organized a joint stock company and started a weekly journal and conducted a job printing establishment. This paper took well and was fast forging to the front as a decided success.

It began to lift up its voice against frauds at the polls and to champion the cause of honest elections. It contended that practicing frauds was debauching the young men, the flower of the Anglo-Saxon race. One particularly meritorious article was copied in *The Temps* and commented upon editorially. This article created a great stir in political circles.

A search was instituted as to the authorship. It was traced to Belton, and the politicians gave the school board orders to dump Belton forthwith, on the ground that they could not afford to feed and clothe a man who would so vigorously "attack Southern Institutions," meaning by this phrase the universal practice of thievery and fraud at the ballot box. Belton was summarily dismissed.

His marriage was of necessity indefinitely postponed. The other teachers were warned to give no further support to Belton's paper on pain of losing their positions. They withdrew their influence from Belton and he was, by this means, forced to give up the enterprise.

He was now completely without an occupation, and began to look around for employment. He decided to make a trial of politics. A campaign came on and he vigorously espoused the cause of the Republicans. A congressional and presidential campaign was being conducted at the same time, and Belton did yeoman service.

Owing to frauds in the elections the Democrats carried the district in which Belton labored, but the vote was closer than was ever known before. The Republicans, however, carried the nation and the President appointed a white republican as postmaster of Richmond. In recognition of his great service to his party, Belton was appointed stamping clerk in the Post Office at a salary of sixty dollars per month.

As a rule, the most prominent and lucrative places went to those who were most influential with the voters. Measured by this standard and by the standard of real ability, Belton was entitled to the best place in the district in the gift of the government; but the color of his skin was against him, and he had to content himself with a clerkship.

At the expiration of one year, Belton proudly led the charming Antoinette Nermal to the marriage altar, where they became man and wife. Their marriage was the most notable social event that had ever been known among the colored people of Richmond. All of the colored people and many of the white people of prominence were at the wedding reception, and costly presents poured in upon them. This brilliant couple were predicted to have a glorious future before them. So all hearts hoped and felt.

About two years from Belton's appointment as stamping clerk and one year from the date of his marriage, a congressional convention was held for the purpose of nominating a candidate for Congress. Belton's chief, the postmaster, desired a personal friend to have the honor. This personal friend was known to be prejudiced against colored people and Belton could not, therefore, see his way clear to support him for the nomination. He supported another candidate and won for him the nomination; but the postmaster dismissed him from his position as clerk. Crushed in spirit, Belton came home to tell his wife of their misfortune.

Although he was entitled to the postmastership, according to the ethics of the existing political condition, he had been given a commonplace clerkship. And now, because he would not play the puppet, he was summarily dismissed from that humble position. His wife cheered him up and bade him to not be despondent, telling him that a man of his talents would beyond all question be sure to succeed in life.

Belton began to cast around for another occupation, but, in whatever direction he looked, he saw no hope. He possessed a first class college education, but that was all. He knew no trade nor was he equipped to enter any of the professions. It is true that there were positions around by the thousands which he could fill, but his color debarred him. He would have made an excellent drummer, salesman, clerk, cashier, government official (county, city, state, or national) telegraph operator, conductor, or any thing of such a nature. But the color of his skin shut the doors so tight that he could not even peep in.

The white people would not employ him in these positions, and the colored people did not have any enterprises in which they could employ him. It is true that such positions as street laborer, hod carrier, cart driver, factory hand, railroad hand, were open to him; but such menial tasks were uncongenial to a man of his education and polish. And, again, society positively forbade him doing such labor. If a man of education among the colored people did such manual labor, he was looked upon as an eternal disgrace to the race. He was looked upon as throwing his education away and lowering its value in the eyes of the children who were to come after him.

So, here was proud, brilliant Belton, the husband of a woman whom he fairly worshipped, surrounded in a manner that precluded his earning a livelihood for her. This set Belton to studying the labor situation and the race question from this point of view. He found scores of young men just in his predicament. The schools were all supplied with teachers. All other doors were effectually barred. Society's stern edict forbade these young men resorting to lower forms of labor. And instead of the matter growing better, it was growing worse, year by year. Colleges were rushing class after class forth with just his kind of education, and there was no employment for them.

These young men, having no employment, would get together in groups and discuss their respective conditions. Some were in love and desired to marry. Others were married and desired to support their wives in a creditable way. Others desired to acquire a competence. Some had aged parents who had toiled hard to educate them and were looking to them for support. They were willing to work but the opportunity was denied them. And the sole charge against them was the color of their skins. They grew to hate a flag that would float in an undisturbed manner over such a condition of affairs. They began to abuse and execrate a national government that would not protect them against color prejudice, but on the contrary actually practiced it itself.

Beginning with passively hating the flag, they began to think of rebelling against it and would wish for some foreign power to come in and bury it in the dirt. They signified their willingness to participate in such a proceeding.

It is true that it was only a class that had thought and spoke of this, but it was an educated class, turned loose with an idle brain and plenty of time to devise mischief. The toiling, unthinking masses went quietly to their labors, day by day, but the educated malcontents moved in and out among them, convincing them that they could not afford to see their men of brains ignored because of color.

Belton viewed this state of affairs with alarm and asked himself, whither was the nation drifting. He might have joined this army of malcontents and insurrection breeders, but that a very remarkable and novel idea occurred to him. He decided to endeavor to find out just what view the white people were taking of the Negro and of the existing conditions. He saw that the nation was drifting toward a terrible cataract and he wished to find out what precautionary steps the white people were going to take.

So he left Richmond, giving the people to understand that he was gone to get a place to labor to support his wife. The people thought it strange that he did not tell where he was going and what he was to do. Speculation was rife. Many thought that it was an attempt at deserting his wife, whom he seemed unable to support. He arranged to visit his wife twice a month.

He went to New York and completely disguised himself. He bought a wig representing the hair on the head of a colored woman.

He had this wig made especially to his order. He bought an outfit of well fitting dresses and other garments worn by women. He clad himself and reappeared in Richmond. His wife and most intimate friends failed to recognize him. He of course revealed his identity to his wife but to no one else.

He now had the appearance of a healthy, handsome, robust colored girl, with features rather large for a woman but attractive just the same. In this guise Belton applied for a position as nurse and was successful in securing a place in the family of a leading white man. He loitered near the family circle as much as he could. His ear was constantly at the key holes, listening. Sometimes he would engage in conversation for the purpose of drawing them out on the question of the Negro.

He found out that the white man was utterly ignorant of the nature of the Negro of to-day with whom he has to deal. And more than that, he was not bothering his brain thinking about the Negro. He felt that the Negro was easily ruled and was not an object for serious thought. The barbers, the nurses, cooks and washerwomen, the police column of the newspapers, comic stories and minstrels were the sources through which the white people gained their conception of the Negro. But the real controlling power of the race that was shaping its life and thought and preparing the race for action, was unnoticed and in fact unseen by them.

The element most bitterly antagonistic to the whites avoided them, through intense hatred; and the whites never dreamed of this powerful inner circle that was gradually but persistently working its way in every direction, solidifying the race for the momentous conflict of securing all the rights due them according to the will of their heavenly Father.

Belton also stumbled upon another misconception, which caused him eventually to lose his job as nurse. The young men in the families in which Belton worked seemed to have a poor opinion of the virtue of colored women. Time and again they tried to kiss Belton, and he would sometimes have to exert his full strength to keep them at a distance. He thought that while he was a nurse, he would do what he could to exalt the character of the colored women. So, at every chance he got, he talked to the men who approached him, of virtue and integrity. He soon got the name of being a "virtuous prude" and the white men decided to corrupt him at all hazards.

Midnight carriage rides were offered and refused. Trips to distant cities were proposed but declined. Money was offered freely and lavishly but to no avail. Belton did not yield to them. He became the cynosure of all eyes. He seemed so hard to reach, that they began to doubt his sex. A number of them decided to satisfy themselves at all hazards. They resorted to the bold and daring plan of kidnapping and overpowering Belton.

After that eventful night Belton did no more nursing. But fortunately they did not recognize who he was. He secretly left, had it announced that Belton Piedmont would in a short time return to Richmond, and throwing off his disguise, he appeared in Richmond as Belton Piedmont of old. The town was agog with excitement over the male nurse, but none suspected him. He was now again without employment, and another most grievous burden was about to be put on his shoulders. May God enable him to bear it.

During all the period of their poverty stricken condition, Antoinette bore her deprivations like a heroine. Though accustomed from her childhood to plenty, she bore her poverty smilingly and cheerfully. Not one sigh of regret, not one word of complaint escaped her lips. She taught Belton to hope and have faith in himself. But everything seemed to grow darker and darker for him. In the whole of his school life, he had never encountered a student who could surpass him in intellectual ability; and yet, here he was with all his conceded worth, unable to find a fit place to earn his daily bread, all because of the color of his skin. And now the Lord was about to bless him with an offspring. He hardly knew whether to be thankful or sorrowful over this prospective gift from heaven.

On the one hand, an infant in the home would be a source of un-bounded joy; but over against this pleasing picture there stood cruel want pointing its wicked, mocking finger at him, anxious for another victim. As the time for the expected gift drew near, Belton grew more moody and despondent. Day by day he grew more and more nervous. One evening the nurse called him into his wife's room, bidding him come and look at his son. The nurse stood in the door and looked hard at Belton as he drew near to the side of his wife's bed. He lifted the lamp from the dresser and approached. An-toinette turned toward the wall and hid her head under the cover. Eagerly, tremblingly, Belton pulled the cover from the little child's face, the nurse all the while watching him as though her eyes would pop out of her head.

Belton bent forward to look at his infant son. A terrible shriek broke from his lips. He dropped the lamp upon the floor and fled out of the house and rushed madly through the city. The color of Antoinette was brown. The color of Belton was dark. But the child was white!

What pen can describe the tumult that raged in Belton's bosom for months and months! Sadly, disconsolately, broken in spirit, thor-oughly dejected, Belton dragged himself to his mother's cottage at Winchester. Like a ship that had started on a voyage, on a bright day, with fair winds, but had been overtaken and overwhelmed in an ocean storm, and had been put back to shore, so Belton now brought his battered bark into harbor again.

His brothers and sisters had all married and had left the mater-nal roof. Belton would sleep in the loft from which in his childhood he tumbled down, when disturbed about the disappearing biscuits. How he longed and sighed for childhood's happy days to come again. He felt that life was too awful for him to bear.

His feelings toward his wife were more of pity than reproach. Like the multitude, he supposed that his failure to properly support her had tempted her to ruin. He loved her still; if anything, more passionately than ever. But ah! what were his feelings in those days toward the flag which he had loved so dearly, which had floated proudly and undisturbed, while color prejudice, upheld by it, sent, as he thought, cruel want with drawn sword to stab his family honor to death. Belton had now lost all hope of personal happiness in this life, and as he grew more and more composed he found himself better prepared than ever to give his life wholly to the righting of the wrongs of his people.

Tenderly he laid the image of Antoinette to rest in a grave in the very center of his heart. He covered her grave with fragrant flowers; and though he acknowledged the presence of a corpse in his heart, 'twas the corpse of one he loved.

We must leave our beautiful heroine under a cloud just here, but God is with her and will bring her forth conqueror in the sight of men and angels.

CHAPTER XII

ON THE DISSECTING BOARD

About this time the Legislature of Louisiana passed a law designed to prevent white people from teaching in schools conducted in the interest of Negroes.

A college for Negroes had been located at Cadeville for many years, presided over by a white minister from the North. Under the operations of the law mentioned, he was forced to resign his position.

The colored people were, therefore, under the necessity of casting about for a successor. They wrote to the president of Stowe University requesting him to recommend a man competent to take charge of the college. The president decided that Belton was an ideal man for the place and recommended him to the proper authorities. Belton was duly elected.

He again bade home adieu and boarded the train for Cadeville, Louisiana. Belton's journey was devoid of special interest until he arrived within the borders of the state. At that time the law providing separate coaches for colored and white people had not been enacted by any of the Southern States. But in some of them the whites had an unwritten but inexorable law, to the effect that no Negro should be allowed to ride in a first-class coach. Louisiana was one of these states, but Belton did not know this. So, being in a first-class coach when he entered Louisiana, he did not get up and go into a second-class coach. The train was speeding along and Belton was quietly reading a newspaper. Now and then he would look out of a window at the pine tree forest near the track. The bed of the railway had been elevated some two or three feet above the ground, and to get the dirt necessary to elevate it a sort of trench had been dug, and ran along beside the track. The rain had been falling very copiously for the two or three days previous, and the ditch was full of muddy water. Belton's eyes would now and then fall on this water as they sped along.

In the meanwhile the train began to get full, passengers getting on at each station. At length the coach was nearly filled. A white lady entered, and not at once seeing a vacant seat, paused a few seconds to look about for one. She soon espied an unoccupied seat. She proceeded to it, but her slight difficulty had been noted by the white passengers.

Belton happened to glance around and saw a group of white men in an eager, animated conversation, and looking in his direction now and then as they talked. He paid no especial attention to this, however, and kept on reading. Before he was aware of what was going on, he was surrounded by a group of angry men. He stood up in surprise to discover its meaning. "Get out of this coach. We don't allow niggers in first-class coaches. Get out at once," said their spokesman.

"Show me your authority to order me out, sir," said Belton firmly.

"We are our own authority, as you will soon find out if you don't get out of here."

"I propose," said Belton, "to stay right in this coach as long ———"

He did not finish the sentence, for rough fingers were clutching his throat. The whole group was upon him in an instant and he was soon overpowered. They dragged him into the aisle, and, some at his head and others at his feet, lifted him and bore him to the door. The train was speeding along at a rapid rate. Belton grew somewhat quiet in his struggling, thinking to renew it in the second-class coach, whither he supposed they were carrying him. But when they got to the platform, instead of carrying him across they tossed him off the train into that muddy ditch at which Belton had been looking. His body and feet fell into the water while his head buried itself in the soft clay bed.

The train was speeding on and Belton eventually succeeded in extricating himself from his bed of mud and water. Covered from head to foot with red clay, the president-elect of Cadeville College walked down to the next station, two miles away. There he found his satchel, left by the conductor of the train. He remained at this station until the afternoon, when another train passed. This time he entered the second-class coach and rode unmolested to Monroe, Louisiana. There he was to have changed cars for Cadeville. The morning train, the one from which he was thrown, made connection with the Cadeville train, but the afternoon train did not. So he was under the necessity of remaining over night in the city of Monroe, a place of some twenty thousand inhabitants.

Being hungry, he went forth in quest of a meal. He entered a restaurant and asked the white man whom he saw behind the counter for a meal. The white man stepped into a small adjoining room to fill the order, and Belton sat down on a high stool at the eating counter. The white man soon returned with some articles of food in a paper bag. Seeing Belton sitting down, he cried out: "Get up from there, you nigger. It would cost me a hundred dollars for you to be seen sitting there."

Belton looked up in astonishment. "Do you mean to say that I must stand up here and eat?" he asked.

"No, I don't mean any such thing. You must go out of here to eat."

"Then," replied Belton, "I shall politely leave your food on your hands if I cannot be allowed to eat in here."

"I guess you won't," the man replied. "I have cut this ham off for you and you have got to take it."

Belton, remembering his experience earlier in the day, began to move toward the door to leave. The man seized a whistle and in an instant two or three policemen came running, followed by a crowd. Belton stood still to await developments. The clerk said to the policeman: "This high-toned nigger bought a meal of me and because I would not let him sit down and eat like white people he refused to pay me."

The officers turned to Belton and said: "Pay that man what you owe him."

Belton replied: "I owe him nothing. He refuses to accommodate me, and I therefore owe him nothing."

"Come along with me, sir. Consider yourself under arrest."

Wondering what kind of a country he had entered, Belton followed the officer and incredible as it may seem, was locked up in jail for the night. The next morning he was arraigned before the mayor, whom the officer had evidently posted before the opening of court. Belton was fined five dollars for vagrancy and was ordered to leave town within five hours. He paid his fine and boarded the train for Cadeville.

As the train pulled in for Cadeville, a group of white men were seen standing on the platform. One of them was a thin, scrawny looking man with a long beard, very, very white. His body was slightly stooping forward, and whenever he looked at you he had the appearance of bending as if to see you better. When Belton stepped on to the platform this man, who was the village doctor, looked at him keenly.

Belton was a fine specimen of physical manhood. His limbs were well formed, well proportioned and seemed as strong as oak. His manly appearance always excited interest wherever he was seen. The doctor's eyes followed him cadaverously. He went up to the postmaster, a short man with a large head. The postmaster was president of the band of "Nigger Rulers" of that section.

The doctor said to the postmaster: "I'll be durned if that ain't the finest lookin' darkey I ever put my eye on. If I could get his body to dissect, I'd give one of the finest kegs of whiskey in my cellar."

The postmaster looked at Belton and said: "Zakeland," for such was the doctor's name, "you are right. He is a fine looking chap, and he looks a little tony. If we 'nigger rulers' are ever called in to attend to him we will not burn him nor shoot him to pieces. We will kill him kinder decent and let you have him to dissect. I shall not fail to call for that whiskey to treat the boys." So saying they parted.

Belton did not hear this murderous conversation respecting himself. He was joyfully received by the colored people of Cadeville, to whom he related his experiences. They looked at him as though he was a superior being bearing a charmed life, having escaped being killed. It did not come to their minds to be surprised at the treatment accorded him for what he had done. Their wonder was as to how he got off so easily.

Belton took charge of the school and began the faithful performance of his duties. He decided to add an industrial department to his school and traveled over the state and secured the funds for the work. He sent to New Orleans for a colored architect and contractor who drew the plans and accepted the contract for erecting the building.

They decided to have colored men erect the building and gathered a force for that purpose. The white brick-masons of Monroe heard of this. They organized a mob, came to Cadeville and ordered the men to quit work. They took charge of the work themselves, letting the colored brick-masons act as hod carriers for them. They employed a white man to supervise the work. The colored people knew that it meant death to resist and they paid the men as though nothing unusual had happened.

Belton had learned to observe and wait. These outrages sank like molten lead into his heart, but he bore them all. The time for the presidential election was drawing near and he arose in the chapel one morning to lecture to the young men on their duty to vote.

One of the village girls told her father of Belton's speech. The old man was shaving his face and had just shaved off one side of his beard when his daughter told him. He did not stop to pull the towel from around his neck nor to put down his razor. He rushed over to the house where Belton boarded and burst into his room. Belton threw up his hands in alarm at seeing this man come, razor in hand, towel around his neck and beard half off and half on. The man sat down to catch his breath. He began: "Mr. Piedmont, I learn that you are advising our young men to vote. I am sure you don't know in what danger you stand. I have come to give you the political history of this section of Louisiana. The colored people of this region far outnumber the white people, and years ago had absolute control of everything. The whites of course did not tamely submit, but armed themselves to overthrow us. We armed ourselves, and every night patrolled this road all night long looking for the whites to come and attack us. My oldest brother is a very cowardly and sycophantic man. The white people made a spy and traitor out of him. When the people found out that there was treachery in our ranks it demoralized them, and our organization went to pieces.

"We had not the authority nor disposition to kill a traitor, and consequently we had no effective remedy against a betrayal. When the news of our demoralized condition reached the whites it gave them fresh courage, and they have dominated us ever since. They carry on the elections. We stay in our fields all day long on election day and scarcely know what is going on. Not long since a white man came through here and distributed republican ballots. The white people captured him and cut his body into four pieces and threw it in the Ouachita River. Since then you can't get any man to venture here to distribute ballots.

"Just before the last presidential campaign, two brothers, Samuel and John Bowser, colored, happened to go down to New Orleans. Things are not so bad down there as they are up here in Northern Louisiana. These two brothers each secured a republican party ballot, and on election day somewhat boastfully cast them into the ballot box. There is, as you have perhaps heard, a society here known as 'Nigger Rulers.' The postmaster of this place is president of the society, and the teacher of the white public school is the captain of the army thereof.

"They sent word to the Bowser brothers that they would soon be there to whip them. The brothers prepared to meet them. They cut a hole in the front side of the house, through which they could poke a gun. Night came on, and true to their word the 'Nigger Rulers' came. Samuel Bowser fired when they were near the house and one man fell dead. All of the rest fled to the cover of the neighboring woods. Soon they cautiously returned and bore away their dead comrade. They made no further attack that night.

"The brothers hid out in the woods. Hearing of this and fearing that the men would make their escape the whites gathered in force and hemmed in the entire settlement on all sides. For three days the men hid in the woods, unable to escape because of the guard kept by the whites. The third night a great rain came up and the whites sought the shelter of their homes.

"The brothers thus had a chance to escape. John escaped into Arkansas, but Samuel, poor fool, went only forty miles, remaining in Louisiana. The mob forced one of our number, who escorted him on horseback, to inform them of the road that Samuel took. In this way they traced and found him. They tied him on a horse and brought him back here with them. They kept him in the woods three days, torturing him. On the third day we heard the loud report of a gun which we supposed ended his life. None of us know where he lies buried. You can judge from this why we neglect voting."

This speech wound up Belton's political career in Cadeville. He thanked the man for the information, assuring him that it would be of great value to him in knowing how to shape his course.

After Belton had been at Cadeville a few years, he had a number of young men and women to graduate from the various departments of his school. He invited the pastor of a leading white church of Monroe to deliver an oration on the day of commencement exercises. The preacher came and was most favorably impressed with Belton's work, as exhibited in the students then graduating. He esteemed Belton as a man of great intellectual power and invited him to call at his church and house if he ever came to Monroe.

Belton was naturally greatly elated over this invitation from a Southerner and felt highly complimented. One Sabbath morning, shortly thereafter, Belton happened to be in Monroe, and thinking of the preacher's kind invitation, went to his church to attend the morning service. He entered and took a seat near the middle of the church.

During the opening exercises a young white lady who sat by his side experienced some trouble in finding the hymn. Belton had remembered the number given out and kindly took the book to find it. In an instant the whole church was in an uproar. A crowd of men gathered around Belton and led him out of doors. A few leaders went off to one side and held a short consultation. They decided that as it was Sunday, they would not lynch him. They returned to the body of men yet holding Belton and ordered him released. This evidently did not please the majority, but he was allowed to go.

That afternoon Belton called at the residence of the minister in order to offer an explanation. The minister opened the door, and seeing who it was, slammed it in his face. Belton turned away with many misgivings as to what was yet to come. Dr. Zackland always spent his Sundays at Monroe and was a witness of the entire scene in which Belton had figured so prominently. He hastened out of church, and as soon as he saw Belton turned loose, hurried to the station and boarded the train for Cadeville, leaving his hymn book and Bible on his seat in the church. His face seemed lighted up with joy. "I've got him at last. Careful as he has been I've got him," he kept repeating over and over to himself.

He left the train at Cadeville and ran to the postmaster's house, president of the "Nigger Rulers," and he was out of breath when he arrived there. He sat down, fanned himself with his hat, and when sufficiently recovered, said: "Well, we will have to fix that nigger, Piedmont. He is getting too high."

"What's that he has been doing now? I have looked upon him as being an uncommonly good nigger. I have kept a good eye on him but haven't even had to hint at him," said the postmaster.

"Well, he has shown his true nature at last. He had the gall to enter a white church in Monroe this morning and actually took a seat down stairs with the white folks; he did not even look at the gallery where he belonged."

"Is that so?" burst out the postmaster incredulously.

"I should say he did, and that's not all. A white girl who sat by him and could not read very well, failed to find the hymn at once. That nigger actually had the impudence to take her book and find the place for her."

"The infernal scoundrel. By golly, he shall hang," broke in the postmaster.

Dr. Zackland continued: "Naturally the congregation was infuriated and soon hustled the impudent scoundrel out. If services had not been going on, and if it had not been Sunday, there is no telling what would have happened. As it was they turned him loose. I came here to tell you, as he is our 'Nigger' living here at Cadeville, and the 'Nigger Rulers' of Cadeville will be disrespected if they let such presumptuous niggers go about to disturb religious services."

"You are right about that, and we must soon put him out of the way. To-night will be his last night on earth," replied the post-master.

"Do you remember our bargain that we made about that nigger when he came about here?" asked Dr. Zackland.

"No," answered the postmaster.

"Well, I do. I have been all along itching for a chance to carry it out. You were to give me the nigger's body for dissecting purposes, in return for which I was to give you a keg of my best whiskey," said Dr. Zackland.

"Ha, ha, ha," laughed the postmaster, "I do remember it now. Well, I'll certainly stick up to my part of the program if you will stick to yours."

"You can bet on me," returned Dr. Zackland. "I have a suggestion to make about the taking off of the nigger. Don't have any burning or riddling with bullets. Just hang him and fire one shot in the back of his head. I want him whole in the interest of society. That whiskey will be the finest that you will ever have and I want a good bargain for it."

"I'll follow your instructions to the letter," answered the post-master. "I'll just tell the boys that he, being a kind of decent nigger, we will give him a decent hanging. Meantime, Doctor, I must get out. To-day is Sunday and we must do our work to-morrow night. I must get a meeting of the boys to-night." So saying, the two arose, left the house and parted, one going to gather up his gang and the other to search up and examine his dissecting appliances.

Monday night about nine o'clock a mob came and took Belton out into the neighboring woods. He was given five minutes to pray, at the expiration of which time he was to be hanged. Belton seemed to have foreseen the coming of the mob, but felt somehow that God was at work to deliver him. Therefore he made no resistance, having unshaken faith in God.

The rope was adjusted around his neck and thrown over the limb of a tree and Belton was swinging up. The postmaster then slipped forward and fired his pistol at the base of his skull and the blood came oozing forth. He then ordered the men to retire, as he did not care for them to remain to shoot holes in the body, as was their custom.

As soon as they retired, three men sent by Dr. Zackland stole out of hiding and cut Belton's body down. Belton was not then dead, for he had only been hanging for seven minutes, and the bullet had not entered the skull but had simply ploughed its way under the skin. He was, however, unconscious, and to all appearances dead.

The three men bore him to Dr. Zackland's residence, and entered a rear door. They laid him on a dissecting table in the rear room, the room in which the doctor performed all surgical operations.

Dr. Zackland came to the table and looked down on Belton with a happy smile. To have such a robust, well-formed, handsome nigger to dissect and examine he regarded as one of the greatest boons of his medical career.

The three men started to retire. "Wait," said Dr. Zackland, "let us see if he is dead."

Belton had now returned to consciousness but kept his eyes closed, thinking it best to feign death. Dr. Zackland cut off the hair in the neighborhood of the wound in the rear of Belton's head and began cutting the skin, trying to trace the bullet. Belton did not wince.

"The nigger is dead or else he would show some sign of life. But I will try pricking his palm." This was done, but while the pain was exceedingly excruciating, Belton showed no sign of feeling. "You may go now," said the doctor to his three attendants, "he is certainly dead."

The men left. Dr. Zackland pulled out his watch and said: "It is now ten o'clock. Those doctors from Monroe will be here by twelve. I can have everything exactly ready by that time."

A bright ray of hope passed into Belton's bosom. He had two

hours more of life, two hours more in which to plan an escape. Dr. Zackland was busy stirring about over the room. He took a long, sharp knife and gazed at its keen edge. He placed this on the dissecting table near Belton's feet. He then passed out of doors to get a pail of water, and left the door ajar.

He went to his cabinet to get out more surgical instruments, and his back was now turned to Belton and he was absorbed in what he was doing. Belton's eyes had followed every movement, but in order to escape attention his eyelids were only slightly open. He now raised himself up, seized the knife that was near his feet and at a bound was at the doctor's side.

The doctor turned around and was in dread alarm at the sight of the dead man returned to life. At that instant he was too terrified to act or scream, and before he could recover his self-possession Belton plunged the knife through his throat. Seizing the dying man he laid him on the dissecting board and covered him over with a sheet.

He went to the writing desk and quickly scrawled the following note.

"DOCTORS:

"I have stepped out for a short while. Don't touch the nigger until I come.

"ZACKLAND."

He pinned this note on that portion of the sheet where it would attract attention at once if one should begin to uncover the corpse. He did this to delay discovery and thus get a good start on those who might pursue him.

Having done this he crept cautiously out of the room, leapt the back fence and made his way to his boarding place. He here changed his clothes and disappeared in the woods. He made his way to Baton Rouge and sought a conference with the Governor.

The Governor ordered him under arrest and told him that the best and only thing he could do was to send him back to Cadeville under military escort to be tried for murder.

This was accordingly done. The community was aroused over the death of Dr. Zackland at the hands of a negro. The sending of the military further incensed them. At the trial which followed, all evidence respecting the mob was excluded as irrelevant. Robbery was the motive assigned for the deed. The whole family with which Belton lived were arraigned as accomplices, because his bloody clothes were found in his room in their house.

During the trial, the jury were allowed to walk about and mingle freely with the people and be thus influenced by the bitter public sentiment against Belton. Men who were in the mob that attempted Belton's murder were on the jury. In fact, the postmaster was the foreman. Without leaving their seats the jury returned a verdict of guilty in each case and all were sentenced to be hanged.

The prisoners were taken to the New Orleans jail for safe keeping. While incarcerated here awaiting the day of execution, a newspaper reporter of a liberal New Orleans paper called on the prisoners. He was impressed with Belton's personality and promised to publish any statement that Belton would write. Belton then gave a thorough detailed account of every happening. The story was telegraphed broadcast and aroused sympathetic interest everywhere.

Bernard read an account of it and hastened to his friend's side in New Orleans. In response to a telegram from Bernard a certain influential democratic senator came to New Orleans. Influence was brought to bear, and though all precedent was violated, the case was manœuvred to the Supreme Court of the United States. Before this tribunal Bernard made the speech of his life and added to his fame as an orator. Competent judges said that the like of it had not been heard since the days of Daniel Webster.

As he pleaded for his friend and the others accused the judges of the Supreme Court wept scalding tears. Bernard told of Belton's noble life, his unassuming ways, his pure Christianity. The decision of the lower court was reversed, a change of venue granted, a new trial held and an acquittal secured.

Thus ended the tragic experience that burned all the remaining dross out of Belton's nature and prepared him for the even more terrible ordeal to follow in after years.

CHAPTER XIII

MARRIED AND YET NOT MARRIED

Bernard was now at the very acme of fame. He had succeeded in becoming the most noted negro of his day. He felt that the time was not ripe for him to gather up his wealth and honors and lay them, with his heart, at Viola's feet. One afternoon he invited Viola to go out buggy riding with him, and decided to lay bare his heart to her before their return home. They drove out of Norfolk over Campostella bridge and went far into the country, chatting pleasantly, oblivious of the farm hands preparing the soil for seed sowing; for it was in balmy spring. About eight o'clock they were returning to the city and Bernard felt his veins throbbing; for he had determined to know his fate before he reached Viola's home. When midway the bridge he pulled his reins and the horse stood still. The dark waters of the small river swept on beneath them. Night had just begun to spread out her sombre wings, bedecked with silent stars. Just in front of them, as they looked out upon the center of the river, the river took a bend which brought a shore directly facing them. A green lawn began from the shore and ran back to be lost in the shadows of the evening. Amid a group of trees, there stood a little hut that looked to be the hut of an old widower, for it appeared neglected, forsaken, sad.

Bernard gazed at this lonesome cottage and said: "Viola, I feel to-night that all my honors are empty. They feel to me like a load crushing me down rather than a pedestal raising me up. I am not happy. I long for the solitude of those trees. That decaying old house calls eloquently unto something within me. How I would like to enter there and lay me down to sleep, free from the cares and divested of the gewgaws of the world."

Viola was startled by these sombre reflections coming from Bernard. She decided that something must be wrong. She was, by nature, exceedingly tender of heart, and she turned her pretty eyes in astonished grief at Bernard, handsome, melancholy, musing.

"Ah, Mr. Belgrave, something terrible is gnawing at your heart for one so young, so brilliant, so prosperous as you are to talk thus. Make a confidante of me and let me help to remove the load, if I can."

Bernard was silent and sat gazing out on the quiet flowing waters. Viola's eyes eagerly scanned his face as if to divine his secret.

Bernard resumed speaking: "I have gone forth into life to win certain honors and snatch from fame a wreath, and now that I have succeeded, I behold this evening, as never before, that it is not worthy of the purpose for which I designed it. My work is all in vain."

"Mr. Belgrave, you must not talk so sadly," said Viola, almost ready to cry.

Bernard turned and suddenly grasped Viola's hands and said in passionate tones: "Viola, I love you. I have nothing to offer you worthy of you. I can find nothing worthy, attain nothing worthy. I love you to desperation. Will you give yourself to a wretch like me? Say no! don't throw away your beauty, your love on so common a piece of clay."

Viola uttered a loud, piercing scream that dispersed all Bernard's thoughts and frightened the horse. He went dashing across the bridge, Bernard endeavoring to grasp the reins. When he at last succeeded, Viola had fainted. Bernard drove hurriedly toward Viola's home, puzzled beyond measure. He had never heard of a marriage proposal frightening a girl into a faint and he thought that there was surely something in the matter of which he knew nothing. Then, too, he was racking his brain for an excuse to give Viola's parents. But happily the cool air revived Viola and she awoke trembling violently and begged Bernard to take her home at once. This he did and drove away, much puzzled in mind.

He revived the whole matter in his mind, and thoughts and opinions came and went. Perhaps she deemed him utterly unworthy of her. There was one good reason for this last opinion and one good one against it. He felt himself to be unworthy of such a girl, but on the other hand Viola had frequently sung his praises in his own ears and in the ears of others. He decided to go early in the morning and know definitely his doom.

That night he did not sleep. He paced up and down the room glancing at the clock every five minutes or so. He would now and then hoist the window and strain his eyes to see if there were any sign of approaching dawn. After what seemed to him at least a century, the sun at last arose and ushered in the day. As soon as he thought Miss Martin was astir and unengaged, he was standing at the door. They each looked sad and forlorn. Viola knew and Bernard felt that some dark shadow was to come between them.

Viola caught hold of Bernard's hand and led him silently into the parlor. Bernard sat down on the divan and Viola took a seat thereon close by his side. She turned her charming face, sweet in its sadness, up to Bernard's and whispered "kiss me, Bernard."

Bernard seized her and kissed her rapturously. She then arose and sat in a chair facing him, at a distance.

She then said calmly, determinedly, almost icily, looking Bernard squarely in the face: "Bernard, you know that I love you. It was I that asked you to kiss me. Always remember that. But as much as I love you I shall never be your wife. Never, never."

Bernard arose and started toward Viola. He paused and gazed down upon that beautiful image that sat before him and said in anguish: "Oh God! Is all my labor in vain, my honors common dirt, my future one dreary waste? Shall I lose that which has been an ever shining, never setting sun to me? Viola! If you love me you shall be my wife."

Viola bowed her head and shook it sadly, saying: "A power higher than either you or I has decreed it otherwise."

"Who is he? Tell me who he is that dare separate us and I swear I will kill him," cried Bernard in a frenzy of rage.

Viola looked up, her eyes swimming in tears, and said: "Would you kill God?"

This question brought Bernard to his senses and he returned to his seat and sat down suddenly. He then said: "Viola Martin, you are making a fool of me. Tell me plainly why we cannot be man and wife, if you love me as you say you do?"

"Bernard, call here to-morrow at ten o'clock and I will tell you all. If you can then remove my objections all will be well."

Bernard leaped up eager to get away, feeling that that would somewhat hasten the time for him to return. Viola did not seem to share his feelings of elation. But he did not mind that. He felt himself fully able to demolish any and all objections that Viola could bring. He went home and spent the day perusing his text-book on logic. He would conjure up imaginary objections and would proceed to demolish them in short order. He slept somewhat that night, anticipating a decisive victory on the morrow.

When Bernard left Viola that morning, she threw herself prostrate on the floor, moaning and sobbing. After a while she arose and went to the dining room door. She looked in upon her mother, quietly sewing, and tried to say in a cheerful manner: "Mamma, I shall be busy writing all day in my room. Let no one disturb me." Her mother looked at her gently and lovingly and assured her that no one should disturb her. Her mother surmised that all had not gone well with her and Bernard, and that Viola was wrestling with her grief. Knowing that spats were common to young people in love she supposed it would soon be over.

Viola went upstairs and entered her room. This room, thanks to Viola's industry and exquisite taste, was the beauty spot of the whole house. Pictures of her own painting adorned the walls, and scattered here and there in proper places were articles of fancy work put together in most lovely manner by her delicate fingers. Viola was fond of flowers and her room was alive with the scent of pretty flowers and beautiful roses. This room was a fitting scene for what was to follow. She opened her tiny writing desk. She wrote a letter to her father, one to her mother and one to Bernard. Her letter to Bernard had to be torn up and re-written time and again, for fast falling tears spoiled it almost as fast as she wrote. At last she succeeded in finishing his letter to her satisfaction.

At eventide she came down stairs and with her mother, sat on the rear porch and saw the sun glide gently out of sight, without a struggle, without a murmur. Her eye lingered long on the spot where the sun had set and watched the hidden sun gradually steal all of his rays from the skies to use them in another world. Drawing a heavy sigh, she lovingly caught her mother around the waist and led her into the parlor. Viola now became all gayety, but her mother could see that it was forced. She took a seat at the piano and played and sang. Her rich soprano voice rang out clear and sweet and passers-by paused to listen to the glorious strains. Those who paused to hear her sing passed on feeling sad at heart. Beginning in somewhat low tones, her voice gradually swelled and the full, round tones full of melody and pathos seemed to lift up and bear one irresistibly away.

Viola's mother sat by and looked with tender solicitude on her daughter singing and playing as she had never before in her life.

"What did it mean?" she asked herself. When Viola's father came from the postoffice, where he was a clerk, Viola ran to him joyously. She pulled him into the parlor and sat on his knee stroking his chin and nestling her head on his bosom. She made him tell her tales as he did when she was a child and she would laugh, but her laugh did not have its accustomed clear, golden ring.

Kissing them good night, she started up to her bed room. When at the head of the stairway she returned and without saying a word kissed her parents again.

When she was gone, the parents looked at each other and shook their heads. They knew that Viola was feeling keenly on account of something but felt that her cheerful nature would soon throw it off. But the blade was in her heart deeper than they knew. Viola entered her room, fastening the door behind her. She went to her desk, secured the three letters that she had written and placed them on the floor a few inches apart in a position where they would attract immediate attention upon entering the room. She then lay down upon her bed and put one arm across her bosom. With her other hand she turned on the gas jet by the head of her bed. She then placed this other hand across her bosom and ere long fell asleep to wake no more.

The moon arose and shed its sad, quiet light through the half turned shutters, through the window pane. It seemed to force its way in in order to linger and weep over such queenly beauty, such worth, meeting with such an accursed end.

Thus in this forbidden path Viola Martin had gone to him who said: "Come unto Me all ye that labor and are heavy laden, and I will give you rest."

CHAPTER XIV

MARRIED AND YET NOT MARRIED (CONTINUED)

At ten o'clock on the next day, Bernard called at Viola's residence. Viola's mother invited him in and informed him that Viola had not arisen. Thinking that her daughter had spent much of the night in meditating on whatever was troubling her, she had thought not to awaken her so early. Bernard informed her that Viola had made an engagement with him for that morning at ten o'clock. Mrs. Martin looked alarmed. She knew that Viola was invariably punctual to an appointment and something unusual must be the matter. She left the room hurriedly and her knees smote together as she fancied she discovered the scent of escaping gas. She clung to the banisters for support and dragged her way to Viola's door. As she drew near, the smell of gas became unmistakable, and she fell forward, uttering a loud scream. Bernard had noticed the anxious look on Viola's mother's face and was listening eagerly. He heard her scream and dashed out of the parlor and up the stairs. He rushed past Mrs. Martin and burst open the door to Viola's door. He drew back aghast at the sight that met his gaze. The next instant he had seized her lifeless form, beautiful in death, and smothered those silent lips with kisses.

Mrs. Martin regained sufficient strength to rush into the room, and when she saw her child was dead uttered a succession of piercing shrieks and fell to the floor in a swoon.

This somewhat called Bernard's mind from his own grief. He lay Viola down upon her own bed most tenderly and set about to restore Mrs. Martin to consciousness. By this time the room was full of anxious neighbors.

While they are making inquiry let us peruse the letters which the poor girl left behind.

"MY DEAR, DEAR, HEART-BROKEN MAMMA:—

"I am in the hands of God. Whatever He does is just, is right, is the only thing to be done. Knowing this, do not grieve after me. Take poor Bernard for your son and love him as you did me. I make that as my sole dying request of you. One long sweet clinging kiss ere I drop into the ocean of death to be lost in its tossing waves.

"VIOLA."

"BELOVED PAPA:—

"Your little daughter is gone. Her heart, though torn, bleeding, dead, gave, as it were, an after throb of pain as it thought of you. In life you never denied me a request. I have one to make from my grave, knowing that you will not deny me. Love Bernard as your son; draw him to you, so that, when in your old age you go tottering to your tomb in quest of me, you may have a son to bear you up. Take my lifeless body on your knee and kiss me as you did of old. It will help me to rest sweetly in my grave.

"YOUR LITTLE VIE."

"DEAR BERNARD:—

"Viola has loved and left you. Unto you, above all others, I owe a full explanation of the deed which I have committed; and I shall therefore lay bare my heart to you. My father was a colonel in the Civil War and when I was very young he would make my little heart thrill with patriotic fervor as he told me of the deeds of daring of the gallant Negro soldiers. As a result, when nothing but a tiny girl, I determined to be a heroine and find some outlet for my patriotic feeling. This became a consuming passion. In 18— just two years prior to my meeting you, a book entitled, "White Supremacy and Negro Subordination," by the merest accident came into my possession. That book made a revelation to me of a most startling nature.

"While I lived I could not tell you what I am about to tell you. Death has brought me the privilege. That book proved to me that the intermingling of the races in sexual relationship was sapping the vitality of the Negro race and, in fact, was slowly but surely exterminating the race. It demonstrated that the fourth generation of the children born of intermarrying mulattoes were invariably sterile or woefully lacking in vital force. It asserted that only in the most rare instances were children born of this fourth generation and in no case did such children reach maturity. This is a startling revelation. While this intermingling was impairing the vital force of our race and exterminating it, it was having no such effect on the white race for the following reason. Every half-breed, or for that, every person having a tinge of Negro blood, the white people cast off. We receive the cast off with open arms and he comes to us with his devitalizing power. Thus, the white man was slowly exterminating us and our total extinction was but a short period of time distant. I looked out upon our strong, tender hearted, manly race being swept from the face of the earth by immorality, and the very marrow in my bones seemed chilled at the thought thereof. I determined to spend my life fighting the evil. My first step was to solemnly pledge God to never marry a mulatto man. My next resolve was to part in every honorable way all courting couples of mulatto people that I could. My other and greatest task was to persuade the evil women of my race to cease their criminal conduct with white men and I went about pleading with them upon my knees to desist. I pointed out that such a course was wrong before God and was rapidly destroying the Negro race. I told them of my resolve to never marry a mulatto man. Many had faith in me and I was the means of redeeming numbers of these erring ones. When you came, I loved you. I struggled hard against that love. God, alone, knows how I battled against it. I prayed Him to take it from me, as it was eating my heart away. Sometimes I would appear indifferent to you with the hope of driving you away, but then my love would come surging with all the more violence and sweep me from my feet. At last, you seemed to draw away from me and I was happy. I felt free to you. But you at last proposed to me when I thought all such notions were dead. At once I foresaw my tragic end. My heart shed bloody tears, weeping over my own sad end, weeping for my beloved parents, weeping for my noble Bernard who was so true, so noble, so great in all things.

"Bernard, how happy would I have been, how deliriously happy, could I but have stood beside you at the altar and sworn fidelity to you. Ours would have been an ideal home. But it was not to be. I had to choose between you and my race. Your noble heart, in its sober moments will sanction my choice. I would not have died if I could have lived without proving false to my race. Had I lived, my love and your agony, which I cannot bear, would have made me prove false to every vow.

"Dear Bernard, I have a favor to ask of you. Secure the book of which I spoke to you. Study the question of the intermingling of the races. If miscegenation is in reality destroying us, dedicate your soul to the work of separating the white and colored races. Do not let them intermingle. Erect moral barriers to separate them. If you fail in this, make the separation physical; lead our people forth from this accursed land. Do this and I shall not have died in vain. Visit my grave now and then to drop thereon a flower and a flag, but no tears. If in the shadowy beyond, whose mists I feel gathering about me, there is a place where kindred spirits meet, you and I shall surely meet again. Though I could not in life, I will in death sign myself,

> "Your loving wife,
> "VIOLA BELGRAVE."

Let us not enter this saddened home when the seals of those letters were broken. Let us not break the solemn silence of those who bowed their heads and bore the grief, too poignant for words. Dropping a tear of regret on the little darling who failed to remember that we have one atonement for all mankind and that further sacrifice was therefore needless, we pass out and leave the loving ones alone with their dead.

But, we may gaze on Bernard Belgrave as he emerges from the room where his sun has set to rise no more. His eyes flash, his nostrils dilate, his bosom heaves, he lifts his proud head and turns his face so that the light of the sky may fall full upon it.

And lifting up his hands, trembling with emotion as though supplicating for the strength of a god, he cries out; "By the eternal heavens these abominable horrors shall cease. The races, whose union has been fraught with every curse known to earth and hell, must separate. Viola demands it and Bernard obeys." It was this that sent him forth to where kings were eager to court his favor.

CHAPTER XV

WEIGHTY MATTERS

With his hands thrust into his pockets, and his hat pulled over his grief stricken eyes, Bernard slowly wended his way to his boarding place.

He locked himself in his room and denied himself to all callers. He paced to and fro, his heart a cataract of violent, tossing, whirling emotions. He sat down and leaned his head upon the bed, pressing his hand to his forehead as if to restore order there. While thus employed his landlady knocked at the door and called through the key hole, informing him that there was a telegram for him. Bernard arose, came out, signed for and received the telegram, tore it open and read as follows:

Waco, Texas, ——*18*—

"HON. BERNARD BELGRAVE, M.C.,

"Come to Waco at once. If you fail to come you will make the mistake of your life. Come.

"BELTON PIEDMONT."

"Yes, I'll go," shouted Bernard, "anywhere, for anything." He seemed to feel grateful for something to divert his thoughts and call him away from the scene where his hopes had died. He sent Viola's family a note truthfully stating that he was unequal to the task of attending Viola's funeral, and that for his part she was not dead and never should be. The parents had read Bernard's letter left by Viola and knew the whole story. They, too, felt that it was best for Bernard to go. Bernard took the train that afternoon and after a journey of four days arrived at Waco.

Belton being apprised by telegram of the hour of his arrival, was at the station to meet him. Belton was actually shocked at the haggard appearance of his old play-fellow. It was such a contrast from the brilliant, glowing, handsome Bernard of former days.

After the exchange of greetings, they entered a carriage and drove through the city. They passed out, leaving the city behind. After going about five miles, they came in sight of a high stone wall enclosure. In the middle of the enclosed place, upon a slight elevation, stood a building four stories high and about two hundred feet long and one hundred and eighty feet wide. In the center of the front side arose a round tower, half of it bulging out. This extended from the ground to a point about twenty feet above the roof of the building. The entrance to the building was through a wide door in this tower. Off a few paces was a small white cottage. Here and there trees abounded in patches in the enclosure, which seemed to comprise about twenty acres.

The carriage drove over a wide, gravel driveway which curved so as to pass the tower door, and on out to another gate. Belton and Bernard alighted and proceeded to enter. Carved in large letters on the top of the stone steps were these words: "Thomas Jefferson College." They entered the tower and found themselves on the floor of an elevator, and on this they ascended to the fourth story. The whole of this story was one huge room, devoid of all kinds of furniture save a table and two chairs in a corner. In the center was an elevated platform about ten feet square, and on this stood what might have passed for either a gallows or an acting pole.

Belton led Bernard to the spot where the two chairs and table stood and they sat down. Belton informed Bernard that he had brought him there so that there would be no possibility of anyone hearing what he had to say. Bernard instantly became all attention. Belton began his recital: "I have been so fortunate as to unearth a foul conspiracy that is being hatched by our people. I have decided to expose them and see every one of them hung."

"Pray tell me, Belton, what is the motive that prompts you to be so zealous in the work of ferreting out conspirators among your people to be hanged by the whites?"

"It is this," said Belton: "you know as it is, the Negro has a hard time in this country. If we begin to develop traitors and conspirators we shall fare even worse. It is necessary, therefore, that we kill these vipers that come, lest we all be slain as vipers."

"That may be true, but I don't like to see you in that kind of business," said Bernard.

"Don't talk that way," said Belton, "for I counted upon your aid. I desire to secure you as prosecuting attorney in the case. When we thus expose the traitors, we shall earn the gratitude of the government and our race will be treated with more consideration in the future. We will add another page to the glorious record of our people's devotion by thus spurning these traitors."

"Belton, I tell you frankly that my share in that kind of business will be infinitesimally small. But go on. Let me know the whole story, that I may know better what to think and do," replied Bernard.

"Well, it is this," began Belton; "you know that there is one serious flaw in the Constitution of the United States, which has already caused a world of trouble, and there is evidently a great deal more to come. You know that a ship's boilers, engines, rigging, and so forth may be in perfect condition, but a serious leak in her bottom will sink the proudest vessel afloat. This flaw or defect in the Constitution of the United States is the relation of the General Government to the individual state. The vague, unsettled state of the relationship furnished the pretext for the Civil War. The General Government says to the citizen: 'I am your sovereign. You are my citizen and not the citizen of only one state. If I call on you to defend my sovereignty, you must do so even if you have to fight against your own state. But while I am your supreme earthly sovereign I am powerless to protect you against crimes, injustices, outrages against you. Your state may disfranchise you with or without law, may mob you; but my hands are so tied that I can't help you at all, although I shall force you to defend my sovereignty with your lives. If you are beset by Klu Klux, White Cappers, Bulldozers, Lynchers, do not turn your dying eyes on me for I am unable to help you.' Such is what the Federal Government has to say to the Negro. The Negro must therefore fight to keep afloat a flag that can afford him no more protection than could a helpless baby. The weakness of the General Government in this particular was revealed with startling clearness in connection with the murder of those Italians in New Orleans, a few years ago. This government had promised Italy to afford protection to the property and lives of her citizens sojourning in our midst. But when these men were murdered the General Government could not even bring the murderers to trial for their crime. Its treaty had been broken by a handfull of its own citizens and it was powerless to punish them. It had to confess its impotence to the world, and paid Italy a specified sum of money. The Negro finds himself an unprotected foreigner in his own home. Whatever outrages may be perpetrated upon him by the people of the state in which he lives, he cannot expect any character of redress from the General Government. So in order to supply this needed protection, this conspiracy of which I have spoken has been formed to attempt to unite all Negroes in a body to do that which the whimpering government childishly but truthfully says it cannot do.

"These men are determined to secure protection for their lives and the full enjoyment of all rights and privileges due American citizens. They take a solemn oath, offering their very blood for the cause. I see that this will lead, eventually, to a clash of arms, and I wish to expose the conspiracy before it is too late. Cooperate with me and glory and honor shall attend us all of our days. Now, Bernard, tell me candidly what you think of the whole matter. May I not rely on you?"

"Well, let me tell you just exactly what I think and just what I shall do," thundered Bernard, rising as he spoke. Pointing his finger at Belton, he said: "I think, sir, that you are the most infernal scoundrel that I ever saw, and those whom you call conspirators are a set of sublime patriots; and further," hissed Bernard in rage through his teeth, "if you betray those men, I will kill you."

To Bernard's surprise Belton did not seem enraged as Bernard thought he would be. Knowing Belton's spirit he had expected an encounter after such words as he had just spoken.

Belton looked indifferent and unconcerned, and arose, as if to yawn, when suddenly he threw himself on Bernard with the agility of a tiger and knocked him to the floor. From secret closets in the room sprang six able bodied men. They soon had Bernard securely bound. Belton then told Bernard that he must retract what he had said and agree to keep his revealed purpose a secret or he would never leave that room alive.

"Then I shall die, and my only regret will be that I shall die at the hands of such an abominable wretch as you are," was Bernard's answer.

Bernard was stood against the wall. The six men retired to their closets and returned with rifles. Bernard gazed at the men unflinchingly. They formed a line, ten paces in front of him. Belton gave

Bernard one last chance, as he said, to save his life, by silence as to his plans.

Bernard said: "If I live I shall surely proclaim your infamy to our people and slay you besides. The curse of our doomed race is just such white folks' niggers as you are. Shoot, shoot, shoot, you whelps."

They took aim and, at a command from Belton, fired. When the smoke had lifted, Belton said: "Bernard, those were blank cartridges. I desired to give you another chance. If you consent to leave me unmolested to ferret out those conspirators I will take your word as your bond and spare your life. Will you accept your life at such a low price?"

"Come here and let me give you my answer," said Bernard. "Let me whisper something in your ear."

Belton drew near and Bernard spat in his face and said, "Take that, you knave."

Belton ordered Bernard seized and carried to the center of the room where stood what appeared to be an acting pole, but what was in reality a complete gallows. A black cap was adjusted over Bernard's head and a rope tied to his hands. He was told that a horrible death awaited him. He was informed that the platform on which he stood was a trap door that concealed an opening in the center of the building, that extended to the first floor. He was told that he would be dropped far enough to have his arms torn from his body and would be left to die.

Bernard perceptibly shuddered at the fate before him but he had determined long since to be true to every higher aspiration of his people, and he would die a death however horrible rather than stand by and see aspiring souls slaughtered for organizing to secure their rights at all hazards. He muttered a prayer to God, closed his eyes, gritted his teeth and nerved himself for the ordeal, refusing to answer Belton's last appeal.

Belton gave command to spring the trap door after he had

counted three. In order to give Bernard a chance to weaken he put one minute between each count. "One—— Two—— Three——" he called out.

Bernard felt the floor give way beneath his feet and he shot down with terrific speed. He nerved himself for the shock that was to tear his limbs from his body, but, strange to say, he felt the speed lessening as he fell and his feet eventually struck a floor with not sufficient force to even jar him severely. "Was this death? Was he dead or alive?" he was thinking within himself, when suddenly the mask was snatched from his face and he found himself in a large room containing desks arranged in a semi-circular form. There were one hundred and forty-five desks, and at each a person was seated.

"Where was he? What did that assemblage mean? What did his strange experiences mean?" he asked himself. He stood there, his hands tied, his eye wandering from face to face.

Within a few minutes Belton entered and the assemblage broke forth into cheers. Bernard had alighted on a platform directly facing the assemblage. Belton walked to his side and spread out his hands and said: "Behold the Chiefs of the conspirators whom you would not betray. Behold me, whom they have called the arch conspirator. You have nobly stood the test. Come, your reward awaits you. You are worthy of it and I assure you it is worthy of you."

Bernard had not been killed in his fall because of a parachute which had been so arranged, unknown to him, to save him in the descent.

CHAPTER XVI

Unwritten History

Belton, smiling, locked his arm in Bernard's and said: "Come with me. I will explain it all to you." They walked down the aisle together.

At the sight of these two most conspicuous representatives of all that was good and great in the race, moving down the aisle side by side, the audience began to cheer wildly and a band of musicians began playing "Hail to the Chief."

All of this was inexplicable to Bernard; but he was soon to learn what and how much it meant. Belton escorted him across the campus to the small but remarkably pretty white cottage with green vines clinging to trellis work all around it. Here they entered. The rooms were furnished with rare and antique furniture and were so tastefully arranged as to astonish and please even Bernard, who had been accustomed from childhood to choice, luxuriant magnificence.

They entered a side room, overlooking a beautiful lawn which could boast of lovely flowers and rose bushes scattered here and there. They sat down, facing each other. Bernard was a bundle of expectancy. He had passed through enough to make him so.

Belton said: "Bernard, I am now about to put the keeping of the property, the liberty, and the very lives of over seven million five hundred thousand people into your hands."

Bernard opened his eyes wide in astonishment and waited for Belton to further explain himself.

"Realize," said Belton, "that I am carefully weighing each remark I make and am fully conscious of how much my statement involves." Bernard bowed his head in solemn thought. Viola's recent death, the blood-curdling experiences of the day, and now Belton's impressive words all united to make that a sober moment with him; as sober as any that he had ever had in his life. He looked Belton in the face and said: "May revengeful lightning transfix me with her fiercest bolts; may hell's most fiery pillars roll in fury around me; may I be despised of man and forgotten of my God, if I ever knowingly, in the slightest way, do aught to betray this solemn, this most sacred trust."

Belton gazed fondly on the handsome features of his noble friend and sighed to think that only the coloring of his skin prevented him from being enrolled upon the scroll containing the names of the very noblest sons of earth. Arousing himself as from a reverie he drew near to Bernard and said: "I must begin. Another government, complete in every detail, exercising the sovereign right of life and death over its subjects, has been organized and maintained within the United States for many years. This government has a population of seven million two hundred and fifty thousand."

"Do you mean all that you say, Belton?" asked Bernard eagerly.

"I shall in a short time submit to you positive proofs of my assertion. You shall find that I have not overstated anything."

"But, Belton, how in the world can such a thing be when I, who am thoroughly conversant with every movement of any consequence, have not even dreamed of such a thing."

"All of that shall be made perfectly clear to you in the course of the narrative which I shall now relate."

Bernard leaned forward, anxious to hear what purported to be one of the most remarkable and at the same time one of the most important things connected with modern civilization.

Belton began: "You will remember, Bernard, that there lived, in the early days of the American Republic, a negro scientist who won an international reputation by his skill and erudition. In our school days, we spoke of him often. Because of his learning and consequent usefulness, this negro enjoyed the association of the moving spirits of the revolutionary period. By the publication of a book of science which outranked any other book of the day that treated of the same subject, this negro became a very wealthy man. Of course the book is now obsolete, science having made such great strides since his day. This wealthy negro secretly gathered other free negroes together and organized a society that had a two-fold object. The first object was to endeavor to secure for the free negroes all the rights and privileges of men, according to the teachings of Thomas Jefferson. Its other object was to secure the freedom of the enslaved negroes the world over. All work was done by this organization with the sole stipulation that it should be used for the furtherance of the two above named objects of the society, and for those objects alone.

"During slavery this organization confined its membership principally to free negroes, as those who were yet in physical bondage were supposed to have aspirations for nothing higher than being released from chains, and were, therefore, not prepared to eagerly aspire to the enjoyment of the highest privileges of freedom. When the War of Secession was over and all negroes were free, the society began to cautiously spread its membership among the emancipated. They conducted a campaign of education, which in every case preceded an attempt at securing members. This campaign of education had for its object the instruction of the negro as to what real freedom was. He was taught that being released from chains was but the lowest form of liberty, and that he was no more than a common cur if he was satisfied with simply that. That much was all, they taught, that a dog howled for. They made use of Jefferson's writings, educating the negro to feel that he was not in the full enjoyment of his rights until he was on terms of equality with any other human being that was alive or had ever lived. This society used its influence secretly to have appointed over Southern schools of all kinds for negroes such teachers as would take especial pains to teach the negro to aspire for equality with all other races of men.

"They were instructed to pay especial attention to the history of the United States during the revolutionary period. Thus, the campaign of education moved forward. The negroes gained political ascendancy in many Southern states, but were soon hurled from power, by force in some quarters, and by fraud in others. The negroes turned their eyes to the Federal Government for redress and a guarantee of their rights. The Federal Government said: 'Take care of yourselves, we are powerless to help you.' The 'Civil Rights Bill,' was declared null and void by the Supreme Court. An 'honest election bill' was defeated in Congress by James G. Blaine and others. Separate coach laws were declared by the Supreme Court to be constitutional. State Constitutions were revised and so amended as to nullify the amendment of the Federal Constitution, giving the negro the right to vote. More than sixty thousand defenseless negroes were unlawfully slain. Governors would announce publicly that they favored lynching. The Federal Government would get elected to power by condemning these outrages, and when there, would confess its utter helplessness. One President plainly declared, what was already well known, 'that the only thing that they could do, would be to create a healthy sentiment.' This secret organization of which we have been speaking decided that some means must be found to do what the General Government could not do, because of a defect in the Constitution. They decided to organize a General Government that would protect the negro in his rights. This course of action decided upon, the question was as to how this could be done the most quickly and successfully. You well know that the negro has been a marvelous success since the war, as a builder of secret societies.

"One member of this patriotic secret society, of which we have been speaking, conceived the idea of making use of all of these secret orders already formed by negroes. The idea met with instant approval. A house was found already to hand. These secret orders were all approached and asked to add one more degree and let this added degree be the same in every negro society. This proposition was accepted, and the Government formed at once. Each order remained, save in this last degree where all were one. This last degree was nothing more nor less than a compact government exercising all the functions of a nation. The grand purpose of the government was so apparent, and so needful of attention, that men rushed into this last degree pledging their lives to the New Government.

"All differences between the race were to be settled by this Government, as it had a well organized judiciary. Negroes, members of this Government, were to be no longer seen fighting negroes before prejudiced white courts. An army was organized and every able-bodied citizen enlisted. After the adjournment of the lodge sessions, army drills were always executed. A Congress was duly elected, one member for every fifty thousand citizens. Branch legislatures were formed in each state. Except in a few, but important particulars, the constitution was modeled after that of the United States.

"There is only one branch to our Congress, the members of which are elected by a majority vote, for an indefinite length of time, and may be recalled at any time by a majority vote.

"This Congress passes laws relating to the general welfare of our people, and whenever a bill is introduced in the Congress of the United States affecting our race it is also introduced and debated here.

"Every race question submitted to the United States judiciary, is also submitted to our own. A record of our decisions is kept side by side with the decisions of the United States.

"The money which the scientist left was wisely invested, and at the conclusion of the civil war amounted to many millions. Good land at the South was offered after the war for twenty-five cents an acre. These millions were expended in the purchase of such lands, and our treasury is now good for $500,000,000. Our citizens own about $350,000,000. And all of this is pledged to our government in case it is needed.

"We have at our disposal, therefore, $850,000,000. This money can be used by the Government in any way that it sees fit, so long as it is used to secure the recognition of the rights of our people. They are determined to be free and will give their lives, as freely as they have given their property.

"This place is known as Jefferson College, but it is in reality the Capitol of our Government, and those whom you have just left are the Congressmen."

"But, Belton," broke in Bernard, "how does it happen that I have been excluded from all this?"

"That is explained in this way. The relation of your mother to the Anglo-Saxon race has not been clearly understood, and you and she have been under surveillance for many years.

"It was not until recently deemed advisable to let you in, your loyalty to the race never having fully been tested. I have been a member for years. While I was at Stowe University, though a young man, I was chairman of the bureau of education and had charge of the work of educating the race upon the doctrine of human liberty.

"While I was at Cadeville, Louisiana, that was my work. Though not attracting public attention, I was sowing seed broadcast. After my famous case I was elected to Congress here and soon thereafter chosen speaker, which position I now hold.

"I shall now come to matters that concern you. Our constitution expressly stipulates that the first President of our Government should be a man whom the people unanimously desired. Each Congressman had to be instructed to vote for the same man, else there would be no election. This was done because it was felt that the responsibility of the first President would be so great, and have such a formative influence that he should be the selection of the best judgment of the entire nation.

"In the second place, this would ensure his having a united nation at his back. Again, this forcing the people to be unanimous would have a tendency to heal dissensions within their ranks. In other words, we needed a George Washington.

"Various men have been put forward for this honor and vigorous campaigns have been waged in their behalf. But these all failed of the necessary unanimous vote. At last, one young man arose, who was brilliant and sound, genial and true, great and good. On every tongue was his name and in every heart his image. Unsolicited by him, unknown to him, the nation by its unanimous voice has chosen him the President of our beloved Government. This day he has unflinchingly met the test that our Congress decreed and has come out of the furnace, purer than gold. He feared death no more than the caress of his mother, when he felt that that death was to be suffered in behalf of his oppressed people. I have the great honor, on this the proudest occasion of my life, to announce that I am commissioned to inform you that the name of our President is Bernard Belgrave. You, sir, are President of the Imperium in Imperio, the name of our Government, and to you we devote our property, our lives, our all, promising to follow your banner into every post of danger until it is planted on freedom's hill. You are given three months in which to verify all of my claims, and give us answer as to whether you will serve us."

* * *

Bernard took three months to examine into the reality and stability of the Imperium. He found it well nigh perfect in every part and presented a form of government unexcelled by that of any other nation.

CHAPTER XVII

CROSSING THE RUBICON

Bernard assumed the Presidency of the Imperium and was duly inaugurated in a manner in keeping with the importance of his high office. He began the direction of its affairs with such energy and tactful discretion as betokened great achievements.

He familiarized himself with every detail of his great work and was thoroughly posted as to all the resources at his command. He devoted much time to assuaging jealousies and healing breaches wherever such existed in the ranks of the Imperium. He was so gentle, so loving, yet so firm and impartial, that all factional differences disappeared at his approach.

Added to his great popularity because of his talents, there sprang up for him personal attachments, marvelous in depth. He rose to the full measure of the responsibilities of his commanding position, and more than justified the fondest anticipations of his friends and admirers. In the meanwhile he kept an observant eye upon the trend of events in the United States, and his fingers were ever on the pulse of the Imperium. All of the evils complained of by the Imperium continued unabated; in fact, they seemed to multiply and grow instead of diminishing.

Bernard started a secret newspaper whose business it was to chronicle every fresh discrimination, every new act of oppression, every additional unlawful assault upon the property, the liberty or the lives of any of the members of the Imperium. This was an illustrated journal, and pictures of horrors, commented upon in burning words, spread fire-brands everywhere in the ranks of the Imperium. Only members of the Imperium had access to this fiery journal.

At length an insurrection broke out in Cuba, and the whole Imperium watched this struggle with keenest interest, as the Cubans were in a large measure negroes. In proportion as the Cubans drew near to their freedom, the fever of hope correspondingly rose in the veins of the Imperium. The United States of America sent a war ship to Cuba. One night while the sailors slept in fancied security, some powerful engine of destruction demolished the vessel and ended the lives of some 266 American seamen.

A board of inquiry was sent by the United States Government to the scene of the disaster, and, after a careful investigation of a most thorough character, decided that the explosion was not internal and accidental but external and by design. This finding made war between the United States and Spain practically inevitable.

While the whole nation was in the throes of war excitement, a terrible tragedy occurred. President McKinley had appointed Mr. Felix A. Cook, a colored man of ability, culture and refinement as postmaster of Lake City, South Carolina. The white citizens of this place made no protest against the appointment and all was deemed satisfactory.

One morning the country awoke to be horrified with the news that Mr. Cook's home had been assaulted at night by a mob of white demons in human form. The mob set fire to the house while the occupants slept, and when Mr. Cook with his family endeavored to escape from the flames he was riddled with bullets and killed, and his wife and children were wounded. And the sole offense for which this dastardly crime was perpetrated, was that he decided to accept the honor which the government conferred upon him in appointing him postmaster of a village of 300 inhabitants. It was the color of his skin that made this acceptance odious in the eyes of his Anglo-Saxon neighbors!

This incident naturally aroused as much indignation among the members of the Imperium as did the destruction of the war ship in the bosoms of the Anglo-Saxons of the United States. All things considered, Bernard regarded this as the most opportune moment for the Imperium to meet and act upon the whole question of the relationship of the negro race to the Anglo-Saxons.

The Congress of the Imperium was called and assembled in special session at the Capitol building just outside of Waco. The session began on the morning of April—the same day on which the Congress of the United States had under consideration the resolutions, the adoption of which meant war with Spain. These two congresses on this same day had under consideration questions of vital import to civilization.

The proceedings of the Anglo-Saxons have been told to the world in minute detail, but the secret deliberations of the Imperium are herein disclosed for the first time. The exterior of the Capitol at Waco was decorated with American flags, and red, white and blue bunting. Passers-by commented on the patriotism of Jefferson College. But, enveloped in this decoration there was cloth of the color of mourning. The huge weeping willows stood, one on each side of the speaker's desk. To the right of the desk, there was a group of women in widow's weeds, sitting on an elevated platform. There were fifty of these, their husbands having been made the victims of mobs since the first day of January just gone.

To the left of the speaker's desk, there were huddled one hundred children whose garments were in tatters and whose looks bespoke lives of hardship. These were the offsprings robbed of their parents by the brutish cruelty of unthinking mobs.

Postmaster Cook, while alive, was a member of the Imperium and his seat was now empty and draped in mourning. In the seat was a golden casket containing his heart, which had been raked from the burning embers on the morning following the night of the murderous assault. It was amid such surrounding as these that the already aroused and determined members of the Congress assembled.

Promptly at eleven o'clock, Speaker Belton Piedmont took the chair. He rapped for order, and the chaplain offered a prayer, in which he invoked the blessings of God upon the negro race at the most important crisis in its history. Word was sent, by proper committee, across the campus informing the president that Congress was in session awaiting his further pleasure. According to custom, the president came in person to orally deliver his message.

He entered in the rear of the building and marched forward. The Congress arose and stood with bowed heads as he passed through. The speaker's desk was moved back as a sign of the president's superior position, and directly in the center of the platform the president stood to speak. He was dressed in a Prince Albert suit of finest black. He wore a standing collar and a necktie snowy white. The hair was combed away from that noble brow of his, and his handsome face showed that he was nerved for what he regarded as the effort of his life.

In his fierce, determined glance you could discover that latent fires, hitherto unsuspected even in his warm bosom, had been aroused. The whole man was to speak that day. And he spoke. We can give you his words but not his speech. Man can photograph the body, but in the photograph you can only glimpse the soul. Words can portray the form of a speech, but the spirit, the life, are missing and we turn away disappointed. That sweet, well modulated voice, full of tender pathos, of biting sarcasm, of withering irony, of swelling rage, of glowing fervor, according as the occasion demanded, was a most faithful vehicle to Bernard; conveying fully every delicate shade of thought.

The following gives you but a faint idea of his masterly effort. In proportion as you can throw yourself into his surroundings, and feel, as he had felt, the iron in his soul, to that extent will you be able to realize how much power there was in what is now to follow:

THE PRESIDENT'S MESSAGE

"Two terrible and discordant sounds have burst forth upon the erstwhile quiet air and now fill your bosom with turbulent emotions. One is the blast of the bugle, fierce and loud, calling us to arms against a foreign nation to avenge the death of American seamen and to carry the cup of liberty to a people perishing for its healing draught. The other is the crackling of a burning house in the night's dead hours, the piteous cries of pain and terror from the lips of wounded babes; the despairing, heart-rending, maddening shrieks of the wife and mother; the harrowing groans of the dying husband and father, and the gladsome shout of the fiendish mob of white American citizens, who have wrought the havoc just described, a deed sufficiently horrible to make Satan blush and hell hastily hide her face in shame.

"I deem this, my fellow countrymen, as an appropriate time for us to consider what shall be our attitude, immediate and future, to this Anglo-Saxon race, which calls upon us to defend the fatherland and at the same moment treats us in a manner to make us execrate it. Let us, then, this day decide what shall be the relations that shall henceforth exist between us and the Anglo-Saxon race of the United States of America.

"Seven million eyes are riveted upon you, hoping that you will be brave and wise enough to take such action as will fully atone for all the horrors of the past and secure for us every right due to all honorable, loyal, law-abiding citizens of the United States. Pleadingly they look to you to extract the arrow of shame which hangs quivering in every bosom, shame at continued humiliation, unavenged.

"In order to arrive at a proper conclusion as to what the duty of the hour is, it would be well to review our treatment received at the hands of the Anglo-Saxon race and note the position that we are now sternly commanded by them to accept.

"When this is done, to my mind, the path of duty will be as plain before our eyes as the path of the sun across the heavens. I shall, therefore, proceed to review our treatment and analyze our present condition, in so far as it is traceable to the treatment which we now receive from the Anglo-Saxon.

"When in 1619 our forefathers landed on the American shore, the music of welcome with which they were greeted, was the clanking of iron chains ready to fetter them; the crack of the whip to be used to plow furrows in their backs; and the yelp of the bloodhound who was to bury his fangs deep into their flesh, in case they sought for liberty. Such was the music with which the Anglo-Saxon came down to the shore to extend a hearty welcome to the forlorn children of night, brought from a benighted heathen land to a community of *Christians*!

"The negro was seized and forced to labor hard that the Anglo-Saxon might enjoy rest and ease. While he sat in his cushioned chair, in his luxurious home, and dreamed of the blessedness of freedom, the enforced labor of slaves felled the forest trees, cleared away the rubbish, planted the seed and garnered the ripened grain, receiving therefore no manner of pay, no token of gratitude, no word of coldest thanks.

"That same hammer and anvil that forged the steel sword of the Anglo-Saxon, with which he fought for freedom from England's yoke, also forged the chain that the Anglo-Saxon used to bind the negro more securely in the thralldom of slavery. For two hundred and forty-four years the Anglo-Saxon imposed upon the hapless, helpless negro, the bondage of abject slavery, robbed him of the just recompense of his unceasing toil, treated him with the utmost cruelty, kept his mind shrouded in the dense fog of ignorance, denied his poor sinful soul access to the healing word of God, and, while the world rolled on to joy and light, the negro was driven cowering and trembling, back, back into the darkest corners of night's deepest gloom. And when, at last, the negro was allowed to come forth and gaze with the eyes of a freeman on the glories of the sky, even this holy act, the freeing of the negro, was a matter of compulsion and has but little, if anything, in it demanding gratitude, except such gratitude as is due to be given unto God. For the Emancipation Proclamation, as we all know, came not so much as a message of love for the slave as a message of love for the Union; its primary object was to save the Union, its incident, to liberate the slave. Such was the act which brought to a close two hundred and forty-four years of barbarous maltreatment and inhuman oppression! After all these years of unremitting toil, the negro was pushed out into the world without one morsel of food, one cent of money, one foot of land. Naked and unarmed he was pushed forward into a dark cavern and told to beard the lion in his den. In childlike simplicity he undertook the task. Soon the air was filled with his agonizing cries; for the claws and teeth of the lion were ripping open every vein and crushing every bone. In this hour of dire distress the negro lifted up his voice in loud, long piteous wails calling upon those for help at whose instance and partially for whose sake he had dared to encounter the deadly foe. These whilom friends rushed with a loud shout to the cavern's mouth. But when they saw the fierce eyes of the lion gleaming in the dark and heard his fearful growl, this loud shout suddenly died away into a feeble, cowardly whimper, and these boastful creatures at the crackling of a dry twig turned and scampered away like so many jackrabbits.

"Having thus briefly reviewed our past treatment at the hand of the Anglo-Saxon, we now proceed to consider the treatment which we receive at his hands to-day.

THE INDUSTRIAL SITUATION

"During the long period of slavery the Negro race was not allowed to use the mind as a weapon in the great 'battle for bread.'

"The Anglo-Saxon said to the negro, in most haughty tones: 'In this great "battle for bread," you must supply the brute force while I will supply the brain. If you attempt to use your brain I will kill you; and before I will stoop so low as to use my own physical power to earn my daily bread I will kill myself.'

"This edict of the Anglo-Saxon race, issued in the days of slavery, is yet in force in a slightly modified form.

"He yet flees from physical exertion as though it were the leprosy itself, and yet, violently pushes the negro into that from which he has so precipitately fled, crying in a loud voice, 'unclean, unclean.'

"If forced by circumstances to resort to manual labor, he chooses the higher forms of this, where skill is the main factor. But he will not labor even here with the negro, but drives him out and bars the door.

"He will contribute the public funds to educate the negro and then exert every possible influence to keep the negro from earning a livelihood by means of that education.

"It is true, that in the goodness of his heart he will allow the negro community to have a negro preacher, teacher, doctor, pharmacist and jackleg lawyer, but further than this he will not go. Practically all of the other higher forms of labor are hermetically sealed so far as the negro is concerned.

"Thus, like Tantalus of old, we are placed in streams of water up to our necks, but when we stoop down to drink thereof the waters recede; lucious fruit, tempting to the eye and pleasing to the taste, is placed above our heads, only to be wafted away by the winds of prejudice, when, like Tantalus we reach up to grasp and eat.

OUR CIVIL RIGHTS

"An Italian, a Frenchman, a German, a Russian, a Chinaman and a Swede come, let us suppose, on a visit to our country.

"As they draw near our public parks they look up and see placards forbidding somebody to enter these places. They pause to read the signs to see who it is that is forbidden to enter.

"Unable to understand our language, they see a negro child returning from school and they call the child to read and interpret the placard. It reads thus: 'Negroes and dogs not allowed in here.'

"The little negro child, whose father's sweaty, unrequited toil cleared the spot whereon the park now stands, loiters outside of the wicker gate in company with the dogs of the foreigners and gazes wistfully through the cracks at the children of these strangers sporting on the lawn.

"This is but a fair sample of the treatment which our race receives everywhere in the South.

"If we enter a place where a sign tells us that the public is served, we do not know whether we are to be waited upon or driven out like dogs.

"And the most shameful and hopeless feature connected with the question of our civil rights is that the Supreme Court has lent its official sanction to all such acts of discrimination. The highest court in the land is the chief bulwark of caste prejudice in democratic America.

EDUCATION

"The race that thinks of us and treats us as we have just indicated has absolute charge of the education of our children.

"They pay our teachers poorer salaries than they do their own;

they give us fewer and inferior school buildings and they make us crawl in the dust before the very eyes of our children in order to secure the slightest concessions.

"They attempt to muzzle the mouths of negro teachers, and he who proclaims too loudly the doctrine of equality as taught by Thomas Jefferson, will soon be in search of other employment.

"Thus, they attempt to cripple our guides so that we may go forward at a feeble pace.

"Our children, early in life, learn of our maltreatment, and having confidence in the unused strength of their parents, urge us to right our wrongs.

"We listen to their fiery words and gaze in fondness on their little clinched fists. We then bow our heads in shame and lay bare to them the chains that yet hold our ankles, though the world has pronounced us free.

"In school, they are taught to bow down and worship at the shrine of the men who died for the sake of liberty, and day by day they grow to disrespect us, their parents who have made no blow for freedom. But it will not always be thus!

COURTS OF JUSTICE

"Colored men are excluded from the jury box; colored lawyers are discriminated against at the bar; and negroes, with the highest legal attainments, are not allowed to even dream of mounting the seat of a judge.

"Before a court that has been lifted into power by the very hands of prejudice, justice need not be expected. The creature will, presumably, serve its creator; this much the creator demands.

"We shall mention just one fact that plainly illustrates the character of the justice to be found in our courts.

"If a negro murders an Anglo-Saxon, however justifiably, let him tremble for his life if he is to be tried in our courts. On the other hand, if an Anglo-Saxon murders a negro in cold blood, without the slightest provocation, he will, if left to the pleasure of our courts, die of old age and go down to his grave in perfect peace.

"A court that will thus carelessly dabble and play in puddles of human blood needs no further comment at my hands.

MOB LAW

"The courts of the land are the facile instruments of the Anglo-Saxon race. They register its will as faithfully as the thermometer does the slightest caprice of the weather. And yet, the poor boon of a trial in even such courts as these is denied the negro, even when his character is being painted with hell's black ink and charges that threaten his life are being laid at his door. He is allowed no chance to clear his name; no opportunity to bid a friend good bye; no time to formulate a prayer to God.

"About this way of dealing with criminals there are three horrible features: First, innocent men are often slain and forced to sleep eternally in dishonored graves. Secondly, when men who are innocent are thus slain the real culprits are left behind to repeat their deeds and thus continue to bring reproach upon the race to which they belong. Thirdly, illegal execution always begets sympathy in the hearts of our people for a criminal, however dastardly may be his crime. Thus the execution loses all of its moral force as a deterrent. That wrath, that eloquence, which would all be used in abuse of the criminal is divided between him and his lynchers. Thus the crime for which the man suffers, is not dwelt upon with that unanimity to make it sufficiently odious, and, as a consequence, lynching increases crime. And, too, under the operation of the lynch-law the criminal knows that any old tramp is just as liable as himself to be seized and hanged.

"This accursed practice, instead of decreasing, grows in extent year by year. Since the close of the Civil War no less than sixty thousand of our comrades, innocent of all crime, have been hurried to their graves by angry mobs, and to-day their widows and orphans and their own departed spirits cry out to you to avenge their wrongs.

"Woe unto that race, whom the tears of the widows, the cries of starving orphans, the groans of the innocent dying, and the gaping wounds of those unjustly slain, accuse before a righteous God!

POLITICS

" 'Governments are instituted among men, deriving their just powers from the consent of the governed!'

"These words were penned by the man whom the South has taught us to revere as the greatest and noblest American statesman, whether those who are now alive or those who are dead. We speak of Thomas Jefferson. They have taught us that he was too wise to err and that his sayings are truth incarnate. They are ready to anathematize any man in their own ranks who will decry the self-evident truths which he uttered.

"The Bible which the white people gave us, teaches us that we are men. The Declaration of Independence, which we behold them wearing over their hearts, tells us that all men are created equal. If, as the Bible says, we are men; if, as Jefferson says, all men are equal; if, as he further states, governments derive all just powers from the consent of the governed, then it follows that the American government is in duty bound to seek to know our will as respects the laws and the men who are to govern us.

"But instead of seeking to know our will, they employ every device that human ingenuity can contrive to prevent us from expressing our opinion. The monarchial trait seems not to have left their blood. They have apparently chosen our race as an empire, and each Anglo-Saxon regards himself as a petty king, and some gang or community of negroes as his subjects.

"Thus our voice is not heard in the General Government. Our kings, the Anglo-Saxons, speak for us, their slaves. In some states we are deprived of our right to vote by frauds, in others by violence, and in yet others by statutory enactment. But in all cases it is most effectually done.

"Burdens may be put upon our shoulders that are weighing us down, but we have no means of protesting. Men who administer the laws may discriminate against us to an outrageous degree, but we have no power to remove or to punish them.

"Like lean, hungry dogs, we must crouch beneath our master's table and snap eagerly at the crumbs that fall. If in our scramble for these crumbs we make too much noise, we are violently kicked and driven out of doors, where, in the sleet and snow, we must whimper and whine until late the next morning when the cook opens the door and we can then crouch down in the corner of the kitchen.

"Oh! my Comrades, we cannot longer endure our shame and misery!

"We can no longer lay supinely down upon our backs and let oppression dig his iron heel in our upturned pleading face until, perchance, the pity of a bystander may meekly request him to desist.

"Fellow Countrymen, we must be free. The sun that bathes our land in light yet rises and sets upon a race of slaves.

"The question remaining before us, then, is, How we are to obtain this freedom? In olden times, revolutions were effected by the sword and spear. In modern times the ballot has been used for that purpose. But the ballot has been snatched from our hands. The modern implement of revolutions has been denied us. I need not say more. Your minds will lead you to the only gate left open.

"But this much I will say: let not so light, so common, so universal a thing as that which we call death be allowed to frighten you from the path that leads to true liberty and absolute equality. Let that which under any circumstances must come to one and all be no terror to you.

"To the martyr, who perishes in freedom's cause, death comes with a beauteous smile and with most tender touch. But to the man whose blood is nothing but sour swill; who prefers to stay like fattening swine until pronounced fit for the butcher's knife; to such, death comes with a most horrifying visage, and seizing the victim with cold and clammy hands hurries with his disgusting load to some far away dumping ground.

"How glad am I that I can glance over this audience and see written upon your faces utter disdain of death.

"In concluding let me say, I congratulate you that after years of suffering and disunion our faces are now *all* turned toward the golden shores of liberty's lovely land.

"Some tell us that a sea is in our way, so deep that we cannot cross. Let us answer back in joyful tones as our vessels push out from the shore, that our clotted blood, shed in the middle of the sea, will float to the other side, even if we do not reach there ourselves.

"Others tell us that towering, snow-capped mountains enclose the land. To this we answer, if we die on the mountain-side, we shall be shrouded in sheets of whitest snow, and all generations of men yet to come upon the earth will have to gaze upward in order to see our whitened forms.

"Let us then, at all hazards, strike a blow for freedom. If it calls for a Thermopylæ, be free. If it calls for a Valley Forge, be free. If contending for our rights, given unto us by God, causes us to be slain, let us perish on the field of battle, singing as we pass out of the world, 'Sweet Freedom's song,' though every word of this soul-inspiring hymn must come forth wrapped in our hearts' warm blood.

"Gentlemen of the Imperium in Imperio, I await your pleasure."

CHAPTER XVIII

The Storm's Master

When Bernard ceased speaking and took his seat the house was as silent as a graveyard. All felt that the time for words had passed and the next and only thing in order was a deed.

Each man seemed determined to keep his seat and remain silent until he had some definite plan to suggest. At length one man, somewhat aged, arose and spoke as follows:

"Fellow citizens, our condition is indeed past enduring and we must find a remedy. I have spent the major portion of my life in close study of this subject, searching for a solution. My impression is that the negro will never leave this country. The day for the wholesale exodus of nations is past. We must, then, remain here. As long as we remain here as a separate and distinct race we shall continue to be oppressed. We must lose our identity. I, therefore, urge that we abandon the idea of becoming anything noteworthy as a separate and distinct race and send the word forth that we amalgamate."

When the word "amalgamate" escaped his lips a storm of hisses and jeers drowned further speech and he quickly crouched down in his seat. Another arose and advocated emigration to the African Congo Free State. He pointed out that this State, great in area and rich in resources, was in the hands of the weak kingdom of Belgium and could be wrested from Belgium with the greatest ease. In fact, it might be possible to purchase it, as it was the personal property of King Leopold.

He further stated that one of his chief reasons for suggesting emigration was that it would be a terrible blow to the South. The proud Southerner would then have his own forests to fell and fields to tend. He pictured the haughty Southern lady at last the queen of her own kitchen. He then called attention to the loss of influence and prestige which the South would sustain in the nation. By losing nearly one half of its population the South's representation in Congress would be reduced to such a point that the South would have no appreciable influence on legislation for one half a century to come. He called attention to the business depression that would ensue when the southern supply merchant lost such an extensive consumer as the negro.

He wound up by urging the Imperium to go where they would enjoy all the rights of free men, and by picturing the demoralization and ruin of the South when they thus went forth. His suggestion met with much favor but he did not make clear the practicability of his scheme.

At length a bold speaker arose who was courageous enough to stick a match to the powder magazine which Bernard had left uncovered in all their bosoms. His first declaration was: "I am for war!" and it was cheered to the echo. It was many minutes before the applause died away. He then began an impassioned invective against the South and recited in detail horror after horror, for which the South was answerable. He described hangings, revolting in their brutality; he drew vivid word pictures of various burnings, mentioning one where a white woman struck the match and ignited the pile of wood that was to consume the trembling negro. He told of the Texas horror, when a colored man named Smith was tortured with a red hot poker, and his eyes gouged out; after which he was slowly roasted to death. He then had Mrs. Cook arise and gather her children about her, and tell her sorrowful story. As she proceeded the entire assembly broke down in tears, and men fell on each other's necks and wept like babes. And oh! Their hearts swelled, their bosoms heaved, their breath came quick with choking passion, and there burst from all their throats the one hoarse cry: "War! war! war!"

Bernard turned his head away from this affecting sight and in his soul swore a terrible oath to avenge the wrongs of his people.

When quiet was sufficiently restored, the man with the match arose and offered the following resolutions:

"WHEREAS, the history of our treatment by the Anglo-Saxon race is but the history of oppression, and whereas, our patient endurance of evil has not served to decrease this cruelty, but seems rather to increase it; and whereas, the ballot box, the means of peaceful revolution is denied us, therefore;

"*Be it Resolved:* That the hour for wreaking vengeance for our multiplied wrongs has come.

"*Resolved* secondly: That we at once proceed to war for the purpose of accomplishing the end just named, and for the further purpose of obtaining all our rights due us as men.

"*Resolved* thirdly: That no soldier of the Imperium leave the field of battle until the ends for which this war was inaugurated are fully achieved."

A dozen men were on their feet at once to move the adoption of these resolutions. The motion was duly seconded and put before the house. The Chairman asked: "Are you ready to vote?" "Ready!" was the unanimous, vociferous response.

The chairman, Belton Piedmont, quietly said: "Not ready." All eyes were then pointed eagerly and inquiringly to him. He called the senior member of the house to the chair and came down upon the floor to speak.

We are now about to record one of the most remarkable feats of oratory known to history. Belton stood with his massive, intellectual head thrown back and a look of determined defiance shot forth from his eyes. His power in debate was well known and the members settled themselves back for a powerful onslaught of some kind; but exactly what to expect they did not know.

Fortunately for Belton's purpose, surprise, wonder, expectancy, had, for the time being, pushed into the background the more violent emotions surging a moment before.

Belton turned his head slowly, letting his eye sweep the entire circle of faces before him, and there seemed to be a force and an influence emanating from the look. He began: "I call upon you all to bear me witness that I have ever in word and deed been zealous in the work of building up this Imperium, whose holy mission it is to grapple with our enemy and wrest from him our stolen rights, given to us by nature and nature's God. If there be one of you that knowest aught against my patriotism, I challenge him to declare it now; and if there be anything to even cast a suspicion upon me, I shall gladly court a traitor's ignoble doom."

He paused here. No one accepted the challenge, for Belton was the acknowledged guiding star that had led the Imperium to the high point of efficiency where Bernard found it.

"By your silence," Belton continued, "I judge that my patriotism is above suspicion; and this question being settled, I shall feel free to speak all that is within me on the subject now before me. I have a word to say in defence of the south—"

"No! No! No! No!" burst from a score of throats. Friends crowded around Belton and begged him to desist. They told him that the current was so strong that it was death to all future usefulness to try to breast it.

Belton waved them away and cried out in impassioned tones:

"On her soil I was born; on her bosom I was reared; into her arms I hope to fall in death; and I shall not from fear of losing popular favor desist from pointing out the natural sources from which her sins arise, so that when judgment is pronounced justice will not hesitate to stamp it with her righteous seal."

"Remember your scars!" shouted one.

"Yes, I am scarred," returned Belton. "I have been in the hands of an angry mob; I have dangled from a tree at the end of a rope; I have felt the murderous pistol drive cold lead into my flesh; I have been accounted dead and placed upon the dissecting table; I have felt the sharp surgical knife ripping my flesh apart when I was supposed to be dead; all of these hardships and more besides I have received at the hands of the South; but she has not and cannot drive truth from my bosom, and the truth shall I declare this day."

Seeing that it was useless to attempt to deter him, Belton continued his speech without interruption: "There are many things in the message of our most worthy President that demand attention. It was indeed an awful sin for the Anglo-Saxon to enslave the negro. But in judging a people we must judge them according to the age in which they lived, and the influence that surrounded them.

"If David were on earth alive to-day and the ruler of an enlightened kingdom, he would be impeached forthwith, fined for adultery, imprisoned for bigamy, and hanged for murder. Yet while not measuring up to the standard of morality of to-day, he was the man after God's own heart in his day and generation.

"If Abraham were here to-day he would be expelled from any church that had any regard for decency; and yet, he was the father of the faithful, for he walked according to the little light that struggled through the clouds and reached him.

"When slavery was introduced into America, it was the universal practice of mankind to enslave. Knowing how quick we all are to heed the universal voice of mankind, we should be lenient toward others who are thus tempted and fall.

"It has appeared strange to some that the Americans could fight for their own freedom from England and yet not think of those whom they then held in slavery. It should be remembered that the two kinds of slavery were by no means identical. The Americans fought for a theory and abstract principle. The negro did not even discern the points at issue; and the Anglo-Saxon naturally did not concern himself at that time with any one so gross as not to know anything of a principle for which he, (the Anglo-Saxon) was ready to offer up his life.

"Our President alluded to the fact that the negro was unpaid for all his years of toil. It is true that he was not paid in coin, but he received that from the Anglo-Saxons which far outweighs in value all the gold coin on earth. He received instruction in the arts of civilization, a knowledge of the English language, and a conception of the one true God and his Christ.

"While all of the other races of men were behind the ball of progress rolling it up the steep hill of time, the negro was asleep in the jungles of Africa. Newton dug for the law of gravitation; Herschel swept the starry sky in search of other worlds; Columbus stood upon the prow of the ship and braved the waves of the ocean and the fiercer ridicule of men; Martin Luther, single handed and alone, fought the Pope, the religious guide of the world; and all of this was done while the negro slept. After others had toiled so hard to give the bright light of civilization to the world, it was hardly to be expected that a race that slept while others worked could step up and at once enjoy all the fruits of others' toil.

"Allow me to note this great fact; that by enslavement in America the negro has come into possession of the great English language. He is thus made heir to all the richest thoughts of earth. Had he retained his mother tongue, it would perhaps have been centuries untold before the masterpieces of earth were given him. As it is we can now enjoy the companionship of Shakespeare, Bacon, Milton, Bunyan, together with the favorite sons of other nations adopted into the English language, such as Dante, Hugo, Goethe, Dumas and hosts of others. Nor must we ever forget that it was the Anglo-Saxon who snatched from our idolatrous grasp the deaf images to which we prayed, and the Anglo-Saxon who pointed us to the Lamb of God that takes away the sins of the world.

"So, beloved fellow citizens, when we calmly survey the evil and the good that came to us through American slavery, it is my opinion that we find more good for which to thank God than we find evil for which to curse man.

"Our President truly says that Abraham Lincoln was in such a position that he was forced to set the negro free. But let us remember that it was Abraham Lincoln and those who labored with him that created this position, from which he could turn neither to the right nor to the left.

"If, in his patriotic soul, we see love for the flag of his country overshadowing every other love, let us not ignorantly deny that other loves were there, deep, strong, and incapable of eradication; and let us be grateful for that.

THE LABOR QUESTION

"Prejudice, pride, self-interest, prompt the whites to oppose our leaving in too large numbers the lower forms of labor for the higher; and they resort to any extreme to carry out their purpose. But this opposition is not an unmixed evil. The prejudice and pride that prompt them to exclude the Negro from the higher forms of labor, also exclude themselves from the lower forms, thus leaving the Negro in undisputed possession of a whole kingdom of labor.

"Furthermore, by denying us clerical positions, and other higher types of labor we shall be forced into enterprises of our own to furnish labor for our own talent. Let us accept the lesson so plainly taught and provide enterprises to supply our own needs and employ our own talents.

"If there is any one thing, more than another, that will push the

Negro forth to build enterprises of his own, it will be this refusal of the whites to employ the higher order of labor that the race from time to time produces. This refusal will prove a blessing if we accept the lesson that it teaches. And, too, in considering this subject let us not feel that we are the only people who have a labor problem on hand to be solved. The Anglo-Saxon race is divided into two hostile camps—labor and capital. These two forces are gradually drawing together for a tremendous conflict, a momentous battle. The riots at Homestead, at Chicago, at Lattimer are but skirmishes between the picket lines, informing us that a general conflict is imminent. Let us thank God that we are not in the struggle. Let us thank Him that our labor problem is no worse than it is.

OUR CIVIL RIGHTS

"For our civil rights we are struggling and we must secure them. But if they had all come to us when they first belonged to us, we must frankly admit that we would have been unprepared for them.

"Our grotesque dress, our broken language, our ignorant curiosity, and, on the part of many our boorish manners, would have been nauseating in the extreme to men and women accustomed to refined association. Of course these failings are passing away: but the polished among you have often been made ashamed at the uncouth antics of some ignorant Negroes, courting the attention of the whites in their presence. Let us see to it, then, that we as a people, not a small minority of us, are prepared to use and not abuse the privileges that must come to us.

"Let us reduce the question of our rejection to a question pure and simple of the color of our skins, and by the help of that God who gave us that color we shall win.

"On the question of education much might be said in blame of the South, but far more may be said in her praise.

"The evils of which our president spoke are grave and must be righted, but let us not fail to see the bright side.

"The Anglo-Saxon child virtually pays for the education of the Negro child. You might hold that he might do more. It is equally true that he might do less. When we contrast the Anglo-Saxon, opening his purse and pouring out his money for the education of the Negro, with the Anglo-Saxon plaiting a scourge to flog the Negro aspiring to learn, the progress is marvelous indeed.

"And, let us not complain too bitterly of the school maintained by the Southerner, for it was there that we learned what true freedom was. It was in school that our hearts grew warm as we read of Washington, of Jefferson, of Henry, apostles of human liberty. It was the school of the Southerner that has builded the Imperium which now lifts its hand in power and might to strike a last grand blow for liberty.

COURTS OF JUSTICE

"As for the courts of justice, I have not one word to say in palliation of the way in which they pander to the prejudices of the people. If the courts be corrupt; if the arbitrator between man and man be unjust; if the wretched victim of persecution is to be stabbed to death in the house of refuge; then, indeed, has mortal man sunk to the lowest level. Though every other branch of organized society may reek with filth and slime, let the ermine on the shoulders of the goddess of justice ever be clean and spotless.

"But remember this, that the Court of last resort has set the example which the lower courts have followed. The Supreme Court of the United States, it seems, may be relied upon to sustain any law born of prejudice against the Negro, and to demolish any law constructed in his interest. Witness the Dred Scott decision, and, in keeping with this, the decision on the Civil Rights Bill and Separate Coach Law.

"If this court, commonly accepted as being constituted with our friends, sets such a terrible example of injustice, it is not surprising that its filthy waters corrupt the various streams of justice in all their ramifications.

MOB LAW

"Of all the curses that have befallen the South, this is the greatest. It cannot be too vehemently declaimed against. But let us look well and see if we, as a people, do not bear some share of the responsibility for the prevalence of this curse.

"Our race has furnished some brutes lower than the beasts of the field, who have stirred the passions of the Anglo-Saxon as nothing in all of human history has before stirred them. The shibboleth of the Anglo-Saxon race is the courage of man and the virtue of woman: and when, by violence, a member of a despised race assails a defenseless woman; robs her of her virtue, her crown of glory; and sends her back to society broken and crushed in spirit, longing, sighing, praying for the oblivion of the grave, it is not to be wondered at that hell is scoured by the Southern white man in search of plans to vent his rage. The lesson for him to learn is that passion is ever a blind guide and the more violent the more blind. Let him not cease to resent with all the intensity of his proud soul the accursed crime; but let this resentment pursue such a channel as will ensure the execution of the guilty and the escape of the innocent. As for us, let us cease to furnish the inhuman brutes whose deeds suggest inhuman punishments.

"But, I am aware that in a large majority of cases where lynchings occur, outrages upon women are not even mentioned. This fact but serves as an argument against all lynchings; for when lawlessness breaks forth, no man can set a limit where it will stop. It also warns us as a race to furnish no crime that provokes lynching; for when lynching once gets started, guilty and innocent alike will suffer, and crimes both great and small will be punished alike.

"In regard to the lynching of our Comrade Cook, I have this to say. Every feature connected with that crime but emphasizes its heinousness. Cook was a quiet, unassuming, gentlemanly being, enjoying the respect of all in a remarkable degree. Having wronged no one he was unconscious of having enemies. His wife and loving little ones had retired to rest and were enjoying the deep sleep of the innocent. A band of whites crept to his house under the cover of darkness, and thought to roast all alive. In endeavoring to make their escape the family was pursued by a shower of bullets and Cook fell to the ground, a corpse, leaving his loved ones behind, pursued by a fiendish mob. And the color of Cook's skin was the only crime laid at his door.

"If ye who speculate and doubt as to the existence of a hell but peer into the hearts of those vile creatures who slew poor Cook, you will draw back in terror; for hell, black hell is there. To give birth to a deed of such infamy, their hearts must be hells in miniature. But there is one redeeming feature about this crime. Unlike others, it found no defense anywhere. The condemnation of the crime was universal. And the entire South cried out in bitter tones against the demons who had at last succeeded in putting the crown of infamy of all the ages upon her brow.

POLITICS

"The South has defrauded us out of the ballot and she must restore it. But in judging her crime let us take an impartial view of its occasion. The ballot is supposed to be an expression of opinion. It is a means employed to record men's ideas. It is not designed as a vehicle of prejudice or gratitude, but of thought, opinion. When the Negro was first given the ballot he used it to convey expression of love and gratitude to the North, while it bore to the South a message of hate and revenge. No Negro, on pain of being ostracised or probably murdered, was allowed to exercise the ballot in any other way than that just mentioned. They voted in a mass, according to the dictates of love and hate.

"The ballot was never designed for such a purpose. The white man snatched the ballot from the Negro. His only crime was, in not snatching it from him also, for he was voting on the same principle. Neither race was thinking. They were both simply feeling, and ballots are not meant to convey feelings.

"But happily that day has passed and both races are thinking and are better prepared to vote. But the white man is still holding on to the stolen ballot box and he must surrender it. If we can secure possession of that right again, we shall use it to correct the many grievous wrongs under which we suffer. That is the one point on which all of our efforts are focused. Here is the storm center. Let us carry this point and our flag will soon have all of our rights inscribed thereon. The struggle is on, and my beloved Congress, let me urge one thing upon you. Leave out revenge as one of the things at which to aim.

"In His Holy Word our most high God has said: 'Vengeance is mine.' Great as is this Imperium, let it not mount God's throne and attempt by violence to rob Him of his prerogatives. In this battle, we want Him on our side and let us war as becometh men who fear and reverence Him. Hitherto, we have seen vengeance terrible in his hands.

"While we, the oppressed, stayed upon the plantation in peace, our oppressors were upon the field of battle engaged in mortal combat; and it was the blood of our oppressor, not our own, that was paid as the price of our freedom. And that same God is alive to-day; and let us trust Him for vengeance, and if we pray let our prayer be for mercy on those who have wronged us, for direful shall be their woes.

"And now, I have a substitute proposition. Fellow Comrades, I am not for internecine war. O! Eternal God, lend unto these, my Comrades, the departed spirit of Dante, faithful artist of the horrors of hell, for we feel that he alone can paint the shudder-making, soul-sickening scenes that follow in the wake of fast moving internecine war.

"Now, hear my solution of the race problem. The Anglo-Saxon does not yet know that we have caught the fire of liberty. He does not yet know that we have learned what a glorious thing it is to die for a principle, and especially when that principle is liberty. He does not yet know how the genius of his institutions has taken hold of our very souls. In the days of our enslavement we did not seem to him to be much disturbed about physical freedom. During the whole period of our enslavement we made only two slight insurrections.

"When at last the war came to set us free we stayed in the field and fed the men who were reddening the soil with their blood in a deadly struggle to keep us in bondage forever. We remained at home and defended the helpless wives and children of men, who if they had been at home would have counted it no crime to have ignored all our family ties and scattered husbands and wives, mothers and children as ruthlessly as the autumn winds do the falling leaves.

"The Anglo-Saxon has seen the eyes of the Negro following the American eagle in its glorious flight. The eagle has alighted on some mountain top and the poor Negro has been seen climbing up the rugged mountain-side, eager to caress the eagle. When he has attempted to do this, the eagle has clawed at his eyes and dug his beak into his heart and has flown away in disdain; and yet, so majestic was its flight that the Negro, with tears in his eyes, and blood dripping from his heart has smiled and shouted: 'God save the eagle.'

"These things have caused us to be misunderstood. We know that our patient submission in slavery was due to our consciousness of weakness; we know that our silence and inaction during the civil war was due to a belief that God was speaking for us and fighting our battle; we know that our devotion to the flag will not survive one moment after our hope is dead; but we must not be content with knowing these things ourselves. We must change the conception which the Anglo-Saxon has formed of our character. We should let him know that patience has a limit; that strength brings confidence; that faith in God will demand the exercise of our own right arm; that hope and despair are each equipped with swords, the latter more dreadful than the former. Before we make a forward move, let us pull the veil from before the eyes of the Anglo-Saxon that he may see the New Negro standing before him humbly, but firmly demanding every right granted him by his maker and wrested from him by man.

"If, however, the revelation of our character and the full knowledge of our determined attitude does not procure our rights, my proposition, which I am about to submit, will still offer a solution.

RESOLUTIONS

"1. Be it *Resolved:* That we no longer conceal from the Anglo-Saxon the fact that the Imperium exists, so that he may see that the love of liberty in our bosoms is strong enough to draw us together into this compact government. He will also see that each individual Negro does not stand by himself, but is a link in a great chain that must not be broken with impunity.

"2. *Resolved:* That we earnestly strive to convince the Anglo-Saxon that we are now thoroughly wedded to the doctrine of Patrick Henry: 'Give me liberty or give me death.' Let us teach the Anglo-Saxon that we have arrived at the stage of development as a people, where we prefer to die in honor rather than live in disgrace.

"3. *Resolved:* That we spend four years in endeavors to impress the Anglo-Saxon that he has a New Negro on his hands and must surrender what belongs to him. In case we fail by these means to secure our rights and privileges we shall all, at once, abandon our several homes in the various other states and emigrate in a body to the State of Texas, broad in domain, rich in soil and salubrious in climate. Having an unquestioned majority of votes we shall secure possession of the State government.

"4. *Resolved:* That when once lawfully in control of that great state we shall, every man, die in his shoes before we shall allow vicious frauds or unlawful force to pursue us there and rob us of our acknowledged right.

"5. *Resolved:* That we sojourn in the state of Texas, working out our destiny as a separate and distinct race in the United States of America.

"Such is the proposition which I present. It is primarily pacific: yet it is firm and unyielding. It courts a peaceable adjustment, yet it does not shirk war, if war is forced.

"But in concluding, let me emphasize that my aim, my hope, my labors, my fervent prayer to God is for a peaceable adjustment of all our differences upon the high plane of the equality of man. Our beloved President, in his message to this Congress, made a serious mistake when he stated that there were only two weapons to be used in accomplishing revolutions. He named the sword (and spear) and ballot. There is a weapon mightier than either of these. I speak of the pen. If denied the use of the ballot let us devote our attention to that mightier weapon, the pen.

"Other races which have obtained their freedom erect monuments over bloody spots where they slew their fellow men. May God favor us to obtain our freedom without having to dot our land with these relics of barbaric ages.

"The Negro is the latest comer upon the scene of modern civilization. It would be the crowning glory of even this marvelous age; it would be the grandest contribution ever made to the cause of human civilization; it would be a worthy theme for the songs of the Holy Angels, if every Negro, away from the land of his nativity, can by means of the pen, force an acknowledgment of equality from the proud lips of the fierce, all conquering Anglo-Saxon, thus eclipsing the record of all other races of men, who without exception have had to wade through blood to achieve their freedom.

"Amid all the dense gloom that surrounds us, this trandscendent thought now and then finds its way to my heart and warms it like a glorious Sun. Center your minds, beloved Congress, on this sublime hope, and God may grant it to you. But be prepared, if he deems us unfit for so great a boon, to buckle on our swords and go forth to win our freedom with the sword just as has been done by all other nations of men.

"My speech is made, my proposition is before you. I have done my duty. Your destiny is in your own hands."

Belton's speech had, like dynamite, blasted away all opposition. He was in thorough mastery of the situation. The waves of the sea were now calm, the fierce winds had abated, there was a great rift in the dark clouds. The ship of state was sailing placidly on the bosom of the erstwhile troubled sea, and Belton was at the helm.

His propositions were adopted in their entirety without one dissenting voice.

When the members left the Congress hall that evening they breathed freely, feeling that the great race problem was, at last, about to be definitely settled.

But, alas! how far wrong they were!

As Belton was leaving the chamber Bernard approached him and put his hands fondly on his shoulders.

Bernard's curly hair was disordered and a strange fire gleamed in his eye. He said: "Come over to the mansion to-night. I wish much to see you. Come about nine P.M."

Belton agreed to go.

CHAPTER XIX

The Parting of Ways

At the hour appointed Belton was at the door of the president's mansion and Bernard was there to meet him. They walked in and entered the same room where years before Belton had, in the name of the Congress, offered Bernard the Presidency of the Imperium.

The evening was mild, and the window, which ran down to the floor, was hoisted. The moon was shedding her full light and Bernard had not lighted his lamp. Each of them took seats near the window, one on one side and the other on the other, their faces toward the lawn.

"Belton," said Bernard, "that was a masterly speech you made to-day. If orations are measured according to difficulties surmounted and results achieved, yours ought to rank as a masterpiece. Aside from that, it was a daring deed. Few men would have attempted to rush in and quell that storm as you did. They would have been afraid of being torn to shreds, so to speak, and all to no purpose. Let me congratulate you." So saying he extended his hand and grasped Belton's feelingly.

Belton replied in a somewhat melancholy strain: "Bernard, that speech and its result ended my life's work. I have known long since that a crisis between the two races would come some day and I lived with the hope of being used by God to turn the current the right way. This I have done, and my work is over."

"Ah, no, Belton; greater achievements, by far, you shall accomplish. The fact is, I have called you over here to-night to acquaint you with a scheme that means eternal glory and honor to us both."

Belton smiled and shook his head.

"When I fully reveal my plan to you, you will change your mind."

"Well, Bernard, let us hear it."

"When you closed your speech to-day, a bright light shot athwart my brain and revealed to me something glorious. I came home determined to work it out in detail. This I have done, and now I hand this plan to you to ascertain your views and secure your cooperation." So saying he handed Belton a foolscap sheet of paper on which the following was written:

A PLAN OF ACTION
FOR THE IMPERIUM IN IMPERIO

1. Reconsider our determination to make known the existence of our Imperium, and avoid all mention of an emigration to Texas.

2. Quietly purchase all Texas land contiguous to states and territories of the Union. Build small commonplace huts on these lands and place rapid fire disappearing guns in fortifications dug beneath them. All of this is to be done secretly, the money to be raised by the issuance of bonds by the Imperium.

3. Encourage all Negroes who can possibly do so to enter the United States Navy.

4. Enter into secret negotiations with all of the foreign enemies of the United States, acquainting them of our military strength and men aboard the United States war ships.

5. Secure an appropriation from Congress to hold a fair at Galveston, inviting the Governor of Texas to be present. It will afford an ex-

cuse for all Negro families to pour into Texas. It will also be an excuse for having the war ships of nations friendly to us, in the harbor for a rendezvous.

6. While the Governor is away, let the troops proceed quietly to Austin, seize the capitol and hoist the flag of the Imperium.

7. We can then, if need be, wreck the entire navy of the United States in a night; the United States will then be prostrate before us and our allies.

8. We will demand the surrender of Texas and Louisiana to the Imperium. Texas, we will retain. Louisiana, we will cede to our foreign allies in return for their aid. Thus will the Negro have an empire of his own, fertile in soil, capable of sustaining a population of fifty million people.

Belton ceased reading the paper and returned it to Bernard.

"What is your opinion of the matter, Belton?"

"It is treason," was Belton's terse reply.

"Are you in favor of it?" asked Bernard.

"No. I am not and never shall be. I am no traitor and never shall be one. Our Imperium was organized to secure our rights within the United States and we will make any sacrifice that can be named to attain that end. Our efforts have been to wash the flag free of all blots, not to rend it; to burnish every star in the cluster, but to pluck none out.

"Candidly, Bernard, I love the Union and I love the South. Soaked as Old Glory is with my people's tears and stained as it is with their warm blood, I could die as my forefathers did, fighting for its honor and asking no greater boon than Old Glory for my shroud and native soil for my grave. This may appear strange, but love of country is one of the deepest passions in the human bosom, and men in all ages have been known to give their lives for the land in which they had known nothing save cruelty and oppression. I shall never give up my fight for freedom, but I shall never prove false to the flag. I may fight to keep her from floating over cesspools of corruption by removing the cesspool; but I shall never fight to restrict the territory in which she is to float. These are my unalterable opinions."

Bernard said: "Well, Belton, we have at last arrived at a point of separation in our lives. I know the Anglo-Saxon race. He will never admit you to equality with him. I am fully determined on my course of action and will persevere."

Each knew that further argument was unnecessary, and they arose to part. They stood up, looking each other squarely in the face, and shook hands in silence. Tears were in the eyes of both men. But each felt that he was heeding the call of duty, and neither had ever been known to falter. Belton returned to his room and retired to rest. Bernard called his messenger and sent him for every man of prominence in the Congress of the Imperium.

They all slept in the building. The leaders got out of bed and hurried to the president. He laid before them the plan he had shown Belton. They all accepted it and pronounced it good. He then told them that he had submitted it to Belton but that Belton was opposed. This took them somewhat by surprise, and finding that Belton was opposed to it they were sorry that they had spoken so hastily.

Bernard knew that such would be their feelings. He produced a written agreement and asked all who favored that plan to sign that paper, as that would be of service in bringing over other members. Ashamed to appear vacillating, they signed. They then left.

The Congress assembled next day, and President Belgrave submitted his plan. Belton swept the assembly with his eyes and told at a glance that there was a secret, formidable combination, and he decided that it would be useless to oppose the plan.

The President's plan was adopted. Belton alone voted no.

Belton then arose and said: "Being no longer able to follow where the Imperium leads, I hereby tender my resignation as a member."

The members stood aghast at these words, for death alone removed a member from the ranks of the Imperium, and asking to resign, according to their law was asking to be shot. Bernard and every member of the Congress crowded around Belton and begged him to reconsider, and not be so cruel to his comrades as to make them fire bullets into his noble heart.

Belton was obdurate. According to the law of the Imperium, he was allowed thirty days in which to reconsider his request. Ordinarily those under sentence of death were kept in close confinement, but not so with Belton. He was allowed all liberty. In fact, it was the secret wish of every one that he might take advantage of his freedom and escape. But Belton was resolved to die.

As he now felt that his days on earth were few, his mind began to turn toward Antoinette. He longed to see her once more and just let her know that he loved her still. He at length decided to steal away to Richmond and have a last interview with her. All the pent up passion of years now burst forth in his soul, and as the train sped toward Virginia, he felt that love would run him mad ere he saw Antoinette once more.

While his train goes speeding on, let us learn a little of the woman whom he left years ago.

Antoinette Nermal Piedmont had been tried and excluded from her church on the charge of adultery. She did not appear at the trial nor speak a word in her own defense. Society dropped her as you would a poisonous viper, and she was completely ostracised. But, conscious of her innocence and having an abiding faith in the justice of God, she moved along undisturbed by the ostracism. The only person about whom she was concerned was Belton.

She yearned, oh! so much, to be able to present to him proofs of her chastity; but there was that white child. But God had the matter in hand.

As the child grew, its mother noticed that its hair began to change. She also thought she discovered his skin growing darker by degrees. As his features developed he was seen to be the very image of Belton. Antoinette frequently went out with him and the people began to shake their heads in doubt. At length the child became Antoinette's color, retaining Belton's features.

Public sentiment was fast veering around. Her former friends began to speak to her more kindly, and the people began to feel that she was a martyr instead of a criminal. But the child continued to steadily grow darker and darker until he was a shade darker than his father.

The church met and rescinded its action of years ago. Every social organization of standing elected Antoinette Nermal Piedmont an honorary member. Society came rushing to her. She gently smiled, but did not seek their company. She was only concerned about Belton. She prayed hourly for God to bring him back to her. And now, unknown to her, he was coming.

One morning as she was sitting on her front porch enjoying the morning breeze, she looked toward the gate and saw her husband entering. She screamed loudly, and rushed into her son's room and dragged him out of bed. She did not allow him time to dress, but was dragging him to the door.

Belton rushed into the house. Antoinette did not greet him, but cried in anxious, frenzied tones: "Belton! there is your white child! Look at him! Look at him!"

The boy looked up at Belton, and if ever one person favored another, this child favored him. Belton was dazed. He looked from child to mother and from mother to child. By and by it began to dawn on him that that child was somehow his child.

His wife eyed him eagerly. She rushed to her album and showed him pictures of the child taken at various stages of its growth. Belton discerned the same features in each photograph, but a different shade of color of the skin. His knees began to tremble. He had come, as the most wronged of men, to grant pardon. He now found himself the vilest of men, unfit for pardon.

A picture of all that his innocent wife had suffered came before him, and he gasped: "O, God, what crime is this with which my soul is stained?" He put his hands before his face.

Antoinette divined his thoughts and sprang toward him. She tore his hands from his face and kissed him passionately, and begged him to kiss and embrace her once more.

Belton shook his head sadly and cried: "Unworthy, unworthy."

Antoinette now burst forth into weeping.

The boy said: "Papa, why don't you kiss Mama?"

Hearing the boy's voice, Belton raised his eyes, and seeing his image, which Antoinette had brought into the world, he grasped her in his arms and covered her face with kisses; and there was joy enough in those two souls to almost excite envy in the bosom of angels.

Belton was now recalled to life. He again loved the world. The cup of his joy was full. He was proud of his beautiful, noble wife, proud of his promising son. For days he was lost in contemplation of his new found happiness. But at last, a frightful picture arose before him. He remembered that he was doomed to die, and the day of his death came galloping on at a rapid pace. Thus a deep river of sadness went flowing on through his happy Elysian fields.

But he remained unshaken in his resolve. He had now learned to put duty to country above everything else. Then, too, he looked upon his boy and he felt that his son would fill his place in the world. But Antoinette was so happy that he could not have the heart to tell her of his fate. She was a girl again. She chatted and laughed and played as though her heart was full of love. In her happiness she freely forgave the world for all the wrongs that it had perpetrated upon her.

At length the day drew near for Belton to go to Waco. He took a tender leave of his loved ones. It was so tender that Antoinette was troubled, and pressed him hard for an answer as to when he was to return or send for them. He begged her to be assured of his love and know that he would not stay away one second longer than was necessary. Thus assured, she let him go, after kissing him more than a hundred times.

Belton turned his back on this home of happiness and love, to walk into the embrace of death. He arrived in Waco in due time, and the morning of his execution came.

In one part of the campus there was a high knoll surrounded on all sides by trees. This knoll had been selected as the spot for the execution.

In the early morn while the grass yet glittered with pearls of water, and as the birds began to chirp, Belton was led forth to die. Little did those birds know that they were chirping the funeral march of the world's noblest hero. Little did they dream that they were chanting his requiem.

The sun had not yet risen but had reddened the east with his signal of approach. Belton was stationed upon the knoll, his face toward the coming dawn. With his hands folded calmly across his bosom, he stood gazing over the heads of the executioners, at the rosy east.

His executioners, five in number, stood facing him, twenty paces away. They were commanded by Bernard, the President of the Imperium. Bernard gazed on Belton with eyes of love and admiration. He loved his friend but he loved his people more. He could not sacrifice his race for his dearest friend. Viola had taught him that lesson. Bernard's eyes swam with tears as he said to Belton in a hoarse whisper: "Belton Piedmont, your last hour has come. Have you anything to say?"

"Tell posterity," said Belton, in firm ringing tones that startled the birds into silence, "that I loved the race to which I belonged and the flag that floated over me; and, being unable to see these objects of my love engage in mortal combat, I went to my God, and now look down upon both from my home in the skies to bless them with my spirit."

Bernard gave the word of command to fire, and Belton fell forward, a corpse. On the knoll where he fell he was buried, shrouded in an American flag.

CHAPTER XX

PERSONAL (BERL TROUT)

I was a member of the Imperium that ordered Belton to be slain. It fell to my lot to be one of the five who fired the fatal shots and I saw him fall. Oh! that I could have died in his stead!

When he fell, the spirit of conservatism in the Negro race, fell with him. He was the last of that peculiar type of Negro heroes that could so fondly kiss the smiting hand.

His influence, which alone had just snatched us from the edge of the precipice of internecine war, from whose steep, heights we had, in our rage, decided to leap into the dark gulf beneath, was now gone; his restraining hand was to be felt no more.

Henceforth Bernard Belgrave's influence would be supreme. Born of distinguished parents, reared in luxury, gratified as to every whim, successful in every undertaking, idolized by the people, proud, brilliant, aspiring, deeming nothing impossible of achievement, with Viola's tiny hand protruding from the grave pointing him to move forward, Bernard Belgrave, President of the Imperium in Imperio, was a man to be feared.

As Bernard stood by the side of Belton's grave and saw the stiffened form of his dearest friend lowered to its last resting place, his grief was of a kind too galling for tears. He laughed a fearful, wicked laugh like unto that of a maniac, and said: "Float on proud flag, while yet you may. Rejoice, oh! ye Anglo-Saxons, yet a little while. Make my father ashamed to own me, his lawful son; call me a bastard child; look upon my pure mother as a harlot; laugh at Viola in the grave of a self-murderer; exhume Belton's body if you like and tear your flag from around him to keep him from polluting it! Yes, stuff your vile stomachs full of all these horrors. You shall be richer food for the buzzards to whom I have solemnly vowed to give your flesh."

These words struck terror to my soul. With Belton gone and this man at our head, our well-organized, thoroughly equipped Imperium was a serious menace to the peace of the world. A chance spark might at any time cause a conflagration, which, unchecked, would spread destruction, devastation and death all around.

I felt that beneath the South a mine had been dug and filled with dynamite, and that lighted fuses were lying around in careless profusion, where any irresponsible hand might reach them and ignite the dynamite. I fancied that I saw a man do this very thing in a sudden fit of uncontrollable rage. There was a dull roar as of distant rumbling thunder. Suddenly there was a terrific explosion and houses, fences, trees, pavement stones, and all things on earth were hurled high into the air to come back a mass of ruins such as man never before had seen. The only sound to be heard was a universal groan; those who had not been killed were too badly wounded to cry out.

Such were the thoughts that passed through my mind. I was determined to remove the possibility of such a catastrophe. I decided to prove traitor and reveal the existence of the Imperium that it might be broken up or watched. My deed may appear to be the act of a vile wretch, but it is done in the name of humanity. Long ere you shall have come to this line, I shall have met the fate of a traitor. I die for mankind, for humanity, for civilization. If the voice of a poor Negro, who thus gives his life, will be heard, I only ask as a return that all mankind will join hands and help my poor downtrodden people to secure those rights for which they organized the Imperium, which my betrayal has now destroyed. I urge this because love of liberty is such an inventive genius, that if you destroy one device it at once constructs another more powerful.

When will all races and classes of men learn that men made in the image of God will not be the slaves of another image?

Reading Group Guide

1. Why do you think Sutton E. Griggs chose to preface his work of fiction with an authoritative statement in which he vouches for Berl Trout's truthfulness? Can you think of other examples of this framing device used in nineteenth-century literature? Consider nonfiction slave narratives, as well as fictional works by authors such as Mark Twain.

2. What motivates Mr. V. M. King, editor of *The Temps*, to pay for Belton Piedmont's college education, and what favor does he ask of Belton in return?

3. Two episodes in chapter 7 are cited by the narrator as having a strong influence on Belton's future: the sermon delivered by Dr. Lovejoy, and the prank involving a pair of dirty socks. How do these two episodes shape Belton's values and affect his adult decisions?

4. How does Griggs portray the subject of miscegenation in *Imperium in Imperio*? Consider the statement by Bernard's father, "I

shall certainly kill myself if I am ever exposed," as well as Viola's motivation for her drastic actions, and the repercussions after Belton's wife gives birth to a light-skinned baby.

5. Belton and Bernard begin their schooling in 1867, shortly after the Civil War has ended. As Griggs follows them through college and into adulthood, what importance do his characters attach to the role that education will play in preparing newly emancipated African Americans for their future lives? Is the system working?

6. "At Stowe University," writes Griggs, "Belton had learned to respect women. It was in these schools that the work of slavery in robbing the colored women of respect, was undone. Woman now occupied the same position in Belton's eye as she did in the eye of the Anglo-Saxon." How would you describe the treatment and perception of African-American women, before and after the Civil War? Judging from the author's depiction of Mrs. Piedmont and Mrs. Fairfax, as well as Viola and Antoinette, how would you characterize his views on the role of women in nineteenth-century American society?

7. Shortly after Belton has arrived in Cadeville, Louisiana, a black villager tells him that their organized fight against white supremacists was lost when his own brother turned traitor, demoralizing and destroying their movement. "We had not the authority nor disposition to kill a traitor," says the villager, "and consequently we had not effective remedy against a betrayal." How does the Imperium in Imperio deal with traitors, and is this drastic punishment justified? How does our present government handle this issue?

8. Summarize the differing positions of Belton and Bernard on what actions the Imperium in Imperio should take in order to obtain full civil rights and equality for African Americans. Is

Belton too conciliatory? Is Bernard too radical, or are his goals justified?

9. Addressing the Imperium in Imperio, Belton declares, "It was indeed an awful sin for the Anglo-Saxon to enslave the negro. But in judging a people we must judge them according to the age in which they lived, and the influence that surrounded them." Do you agree? Can you think of other examples throughout history of nations or communities engaging in behaviors that are now considered barbaric?

Clotel
WILLIAM WELLS BROWN
Introduction by Hilton Als
0-679-78323-7; trade paperback; 256 pp.

The House Behind the Cedars
CHARLES W. CHESNUTT
Edited, with an Introduction and Notes, by Judith Jackson Fossett
0-8129-6616-3; trade paperback; 256 pp.

My Bondage and My Freedom
FREDERICK DOUGLASS
Edited, with a Foreword and Notes, by John Stauffer
0-8129-7031-4; trade paperback; 384 pp.

Narrative of the Life of Frederick Douglass, an American Slave
and *Incidents in the Life of a Slave Girl*
FREDERICK DOUGLASS AND HARRIET JACOBS
Introduction by Kwame Anthony Appiah
0-679-78328-8; trade paperback; 432 pp.

John Brown
W.E.B. DU BOIS
Edited and with an Introduction by David Roediger
0-679-78353-9; trade paperback; 304 pp.

The Collected Essays of Ralph Ellison
PREFACE BY SAUL BELLOW
Edited and with an Introduction by John F. Callahan
0-8129-6826-3; trade paperback; 904 pp.

Living with Music
RALPH ELLISON
Edited and with an Introduction by Robert G. O'Meally
0-375-76023-7; trade paperback; 336 pp.

The Interesting Narrative of the Life of Olaudah Equiano
OLAUDAH EQUIANO
Edited with Notes by Shelly Eversley
Introduction by Robert Reid-Pharr
0-375-76115-2; trade paperback; 320 pp.

Passing
NELLA LARSEN
Introduction by Ntozake Shange
Critical Foreword and Notes by Mae Henderson
0-375-75813-5; trade paperback; 304 pp.

MODERN LIBRARY IS ONLINE AT
WWW.MODERNLIBRARY.COM

MODERN LIBRARY ONLINE IS YOUR GUIDE TO CLASSIC LITERATURE ON THE WEB

THE MODERN LIBRARY E-NEWSLETTER

Our free e-mail newsletter is sent to subscribers, and features sample chapters, interviews with and essays by our authors, upcoming books, special promotions, announcements, and news.

To subscribe to the Modern Library e-newsletter, send a blank e-mail to: **sub_modernlibrary@info.randomhouse.com** or visit **www.modernlibrary.com**

THE MODERN LIBRARY WEBSITE

Check out the Modern Library website at
www.modernlibrary.com for:

- The Modern Library e-newsletter
- A list of our current and upcoming titles and series
- Reading Group Guides and exclusive author spotlights
- Special features with information on the classics and other paperback series
- Excerpts from new releases and other titles
- A list of our e-books and information on where to buy them
- The Modern Library Editorial Board's 100 Best Novels and 100 Best Nonfiction Books of the Twentieth Century written in the English language
- News and announcements

Questions? E-mail us at **modernlibrary@randomhouse.com**
For questions about examination or desk copies, please visit
the Random House Academic Resources site at
www.randomhouse.com/academic